THE
MAKING OF AMERICA
SERIES

DURHAM
A BULL CITY STORY

YOUNG GAYLE MARIE KING OF CREEDMOOR. *She watches the auction season's opening day in Durham on August 8, 1978. Before a decade more would pass, tobacco auctions in Durham would be only history. (Jim Thornton photo, courtesy of* The Herald-Sun.)

FRONT COVER: *EAST DURHAM CONCERT BAND. They struck this pose on July 4, 1910. (Courtesy Duke University Manuscripts Collection.)*

BACK COVER: *MID-1960s VIEW. This photo of the Durham skyline was taken from the south of the American Tobacco factory. (Harold Moore photo, courtesy of the* Herald-Sun.)

THE
MAKING OF AMERICA
SERIES

DURHAM
A BULL CITY STORY

JIM WISE

ARCADIA

Published by Arcadia Publishing,
an imprint of Tempus Publishing, Inc.
2 Cumberland Street
Charleston, SC 29401

Printed in Great Britain.

Library of Congress Catalog Card Number: 2002105029

For all general information contact Arcadia Publishing at:
Telephone 843-853-2070
Fax 843-853-0044
E-Mail sales@arcadiapublishing.com

For customer service and orders:
Toll-Free 1-888-313-2665

Visit us on the Internet at http://www.arcadiapublishing.com

Dedicated to
the legacies of
George and Mary Pyne
and to
Ruby "Mom" Planck
and the Poets' Corner crowd.

CONTENTS

Preface

This book is an exercise in storytelling. The story is constructed of actual events and real people, as well as oral histories, anecdotes, and folktales that are identified as such, but the selection, arrangement, and linking commentary are my own. It is a true story, but it is only one of many Bull City stories that I and others might tell and have told and, if we are wise about our future business, will go on telling as long as there is anyone to read or listen. Maybe longer.

Durham, the idea of this community, is made of many, many stories. Hearing them, sharing them and, yes, embellishing as they go along in the spirit of true folk art, is one of the privileges and joys of living in Durham and being part of its ongoing conversation. Durham is a product of coincidence (which some believe is God's way of working incognito) and unintended consequences. That's what makes the stories so rich, meaningful, and entertaining, and such excellent vessels for our city's truths.

In my roles as critic and commentator over 21 years with the Durham Herald Company, I have been occasionally criticized for writing from a negative point of view. That's OK. Good journalism, good history, good scholarship are all about give and take and interplay in the marketplace of ideas. And those who know me or have followed my work, I think, recognize that I write from a point of great fondness and fun. Through 36 years in Durham, I have found my adopted hometown a wonder-full, rewarding, and fun place to live, and I am blessed to have stumbled upon it—as a hapless Duke University freshman in September 1966—and to have raised children for whom Durham will always be home. There is only one prerequisite for living happily and well in Durham: a sense of humor.

And if you haven't got one of those, you'd be better off in Cary anyhow.

Jim Wise
March 2002

ACKNOWLEDGMENTS

Much of the research behind this book was originally undertaken in my capacity as reporter, editor, and columnist at the *Durham Morning Herald* and *Herald-Sun* newspapers. For encouragement and opportunity, I wish to thank present and former colleagues Jon Ham, Bill Hawkins, Dave Hughey, Bill Stagg, Cameron Tew, Kim Spurr, and Ven Carver, plus Mike Rouse and Jack Adams, for their generosity in granting me a job interview on the opening Saturday of dove season in 1981. Particular thanks also to *Herald-Sun* librarians Janet Sammons, Michelle Rosen, and Mary Clements.

Other research was done in my capacity as instructor in local and Southern history at the Duke Institute for Learning in Retirement. Gratitude to director Sara Craven and to the many DILR members who signed up and kept coming back.

For aid, comfort, patience, and advice along the way, thanks to Lyn Richardson of the Durham County Public Library; Janie C. Morris of the Duke University Rare Book, Manuscript, and Special Collections Library; Tom Harkins of the Duke University Archives; Dale Coats and Jennifer Farley of the Duke Homestead State Historic Site; Davis Waters and Kent McCoury of Bennett Place State Historic Site; Ernie Dollar of the Orange County Historical Museum; Juliana Hoekstra and Kathleen Needham of Historic Stagville; Beth Highley of West Point on the Eno Park; Diane Pledger of the Hayti Heritage Center; and to Curtis Booker, Robert Brown, Ed Clayton, Frank DePasquale, Mary-Jo Hall, Dot Hannen, Alice Jane Eley Jones, and Southgate Jones Jr.

Most of all, gratitude and love to Babs, Elizabeth, and Ben.

Prologue: The Way Things Happen

In the beginning—but no, let's back up for a moment first.

Curing tobacco is sleepy work. Sure, there are traditions of the men and boys sitting up nights to tend the curing fires, passing a jar of clear whiskey, and swapping yarns of coon dogs, big fish, and things that went bump in the night. However, such traditions smack of invention in retrospect, good old days imagined when they were no longer the stuff of necessity. Truth be told, tobacco is a laborious thing to live by, and the curing of it—while one of the many points where everything of the last year's work and the next year's prospects can go absolutely wrong—is more likely a slow, solo, and sleepy occupation.

So it must have been for Stephen.

It was a rainy night, too, in the summer of 1839, and Stephen was an 18-year-old slave on the plantation of Abisha Slade. Slade was a prosperous planter and a man of affairs in Caswell County, North Carolina, a prosperous country of tobacco, fine horses, and commerce just below the Virginia line, with the Dan River along its northern edge and easy access to the Old Dominion's tobacco markets in Danville and Petersburg. Being a man of affairs, Slade left most of the running of his farm to his bright and capable young servant.

Stephen left no account of what was going on in his mind that night, as he watched beside the curing barn. Perhaps he was in love, maybe he had hopes and ambitions. Among his other talents, he was the plantation blacksmith and he must have known that there were opportunities for an African-American man of ability. He had to look no farther than the nearby village of Milton, where the free black cabinetmaker Thomas Day had become a pillar of the community, a businessman and artisan whose craft and status were prized by the state's power brokers and whose daughter could be educated in an otherwise white-only school.

Perhaps he was only thinking over the next day's work. In any case, as the hours inched by and the steady fire lulled his senses, he fell asleep on the job. When he awoke, maybe out of a dream that alarmed him, the curing fire was nearly out.

In his smithy, Stephen kept a goodly supply of charcoal. Suddenly awake, suddenly alert, suddenly shocked and scared and well aware of his dereliction and its possible consequences, he thought fast. He ran to his shop, grabbed up several hunks of charred wood, hurried back, and dumped them onto the failing fire.

The fire caught up with a sudden burst of heat and an unexpected result. The tobacco, which normally cured out brown, was turning yellow. Stephen reminisced about it almost 50 years later: "To tell the truth about it, 'twas an accident. I commenced to cure it and it commenced to git yellow. It kep' on yallowin' and kep' on yallowin' and kep' on yallowin' twell it got clar up . . . It looked so purty. I kept making it yellow and when it was cured it was 'musement for folks to come and see it."

Stephen had created brightleaf tobacco. Six hundred pounds of it, like no one had ever seen, much less smoked or chewed. At the Danville market, that first yellow batch brought $40 per hundred pounds when the going rate for leaf was $10. Dumb luck and quick thinking had started an industry.

Old Adam Trollinger came from the Rhine Valley in 1737 and settled first in Pennsylvania. Then, like innumerable other German immigrants, he took the route west along the wagon road and south through the Shenandoah Valley into piedmont North Carolina. This time he settled on the Haw River, in what would soon become Orange, and later Alamance County.

STEPHEN, A SLAVE BLACKSMITH. He accidentally discovered a technique for curing brightleaf tobacco in 1839 and this discovery was the foundation of an industry. (Courtesy of Duke Homestead State Historical Site.)

ARTELIA RONEY. Reputed to be the prettiest girl in Alamance County, she caught the eye of widower Washington Duke at a revival preached by Duke's older brother Willie. Their youngest son James Buchanan built an empire on tobacco and electric power. (Courtesy of Elon University.)

With eyes toward future opportunity in a region with no more than 20 official owners of property, Adam settled near a ford and his son Jacob built a gristmill nearby. Jacob, in turn, had two sons in the village of Trollinger's Ford, John and Henry. Henry built a toll bridge over the Haw and married Nancy Thomas, sister of renowned evangelist Joseph Thomas, known in his time as the White Pilgrim because he only wore white clothing.

Henry and Nancy had a son, another John Trollinger, who in 1832 built a cotton mill. Textile manufacturing was an infant industry in North Carolina, begun only in the 1820s when the great bulk of the southern staple was sold and shipped to factories in New England. John married Elizabeth Roney and with her fathered 10 children—5 girls and 5 boys. The eldest son Benjamin would go into the cottonmill business himself, building the Granite Cotton Factory above the old river ford in 1844.

In a family of entrepreneurs, Ben Trollinger stood out. When the state of North Carolina undertook to build a railroad connecting the state's interior with its eastern ports, Trollinger bought stock and gained a spot on the board of directors. Thus positioned, he could bring influence to bear when the engineers debated which route to take between Raleigh and Greensboro, so it was no accident that the route chosen lay beside the Granite Cotton Factory. Trollinger even built three trestles to get track to his property.

Ben Trollinger further put together a land deal for the North Carolina Railroad's maintenance shops, which grew into the town of Burlington. He built a hotel at Haw River, which eventually failed and took Trollinger into bankruptcy, but with new ventures in turpentine, railroad building, and salt works, he had all but discharged his debts by the time of his death in 1862. For his acumen and for services to the Confederate cause, Trollinger was laid to rest with the informal honorific of "General" Ben.

More to our point, on January 30, 1856, the North Carolina Railroad opened full service between Goldsboro and Charlotte, going by way of Haw River, Hillsborough, and Morrisville.

Meantime, Henry Trollinger's sister Mary married John Roney, of another old line in the Alamance country. Their daughter Artelia, Ben Trollinger's first cousin, grew up to be called the prettiest girl of the county.

A painting of Artelia suggests a tender heart and events indicate a loving soul. In any case, when she was a belle of 21 or so, she caught the eye of a widower from the next county to the east.

Perhaps Artelia inherited piety from her evangelist ancestor, for tradition holds that she met Washington Duke at a revival preached at Alamance's Pisgah Church by Duke's older brother Willie. Religion would have been a point in common, for the frugal and hard-working farmer had received the Lord as a boy of 10 at the 1830 summer camp meeting at the crossroads of Balltown (later Hunkadora and, still later, Bahama).

Duke was 32 when they married. He already had two children by his deceased first wife Mary Clinton, a farm of close to 300 acres, and a wood-frame homeplace. Artelia took to caring for her two stepsons, 8-year-old Sidney and 6-year-old Brodie (pronounced "Broddy") as if they were her own, and three more children shortly entered the Duke household: Mary Elizabeth in 1853, Benjamin Newton in 1855, and the youngest, Buck—short for James Buchanan—in 1856.

Now the pieces were in place.

1. THE FLOWER OF CAROLINA

Durham, North Carolina, is a town of 187,000 (according to the 2000 U.S. census) in northeastern central, or "piedmont," North Carolina. From its northern limit, Durham is 32 miles below the Virginia state line. Together with the neighboring towns of Chapel Hill, home of the University of North Carolina, to the west-southwest; and Raleigh, the state capital, to the south-southeast, Durham is part of a geographic triangle called the "Research Triangle" region, comprising those three towns and several more including Carrboro, Hillsborough, Morrisville, Cary, Garner, Apex, and Wake Forest. The Triangle metropolitan area had a 2000 population of 1.2 million, reasonably expected to grow to 2 million by the year 2025, driven by an economy of government, medicine, the telecommunication and higher-education industries, and real estate development and speculation.

The city of Durham occupies the southern half of Durham County, a rough rectangle of 296 square miles, 19 miles north-south and from 7 to 12 miles east-west. Durham County was created in 1881, taking the approximate eastern half of Orange County, which remains adjacent on the west, and a corner of Wake County on the southeast. Other counties around Durham are Person to the north, Granville to the northeast, and Chatham to the southwest. Caswell and Alamance Counties are west and northwest, respectively, of Orange County.

Interstate Highway 85 crosses the northern part of the city of Durham, Interstate 40 the south. The Raleigh-Durham International Airport and the Research Triangle Park lie between Durham and Raleigh on opposite sides of the Durham-Wake County line and at the center, literally and figuratively, of the Triangle region.

Durham took form along a ridge at 36 degrees north latitude, 79 degrees west longitude, roughly 150 miles north-northwest from the Atlantic Ocean at Wilmington and 90 miles east-southeast of the Blue Ridge escarpment near Stuart, Virginia.

In more elemental terms, the high ground of Durham separates the Neuse River watershed from that of the Cape Fear River. On the north, the Neuse is formed by the joining of three rivers which, at many points along their courses, would anywhere else be called creeks: the Flat, the Little, and the Eno, reading north to south. South of the ridge, the only waterway of consequence is New Hope Creek, which flowed (before construction of the B. Everett Jordan Reservoir in the 1970s) into the Haw River and thence the Cape Fear.

Earliest settlement in the region occurred along those streams and their tributaries and the earliest commerce occurred along a network of foot trails that linked reliable fording points. In times to come, those foot trails would grow into pack-horse and then wagon routes extending from the James River to the Savannah, known as the Indian Trading Path and roughly paralleled by present-day rail and highways. But that was all to come.

In the beginning—say, 600 million years ago—this region was the bed of a sea studded with volcanic islands. In 1975, Virginia Tech geologist Lynn Glover found fossil imprints of Precambrian worms supposed to have lived along those islands' shores, the oldest fossils found to that time in the Western Hemisphere. They had rested along the Little River, northwest of the present city, as part of a geological formation called the Carolina Slate Belt.

Durham's ridge, however, runs through a formation 400 million years more recent, the Triassic Basin. That basin underlies the southeastern two-thirds of Durham County and almost all of the city of Durham. This geology creates a hilly upland north and northwest of town, peaking at 730 feet above sea level near the intersection of Guess and Milton roads, and an undulating sweep of ridges and

NATIVES OF COASTAL NORTH CAROLINA. This sixteenth-century engraving was done by Theodore de Bry after a 1584 watercolor by John White, a scholar employed for three expeditions sponsored by Sir Walter Raleigh. (Courtesy of North Carolina Division of Archives and History.)

gullies dropping toward a low point of 230 feet above sea level near Stagecoach and Farrington Roads in the sandy and marshy south.

Soils in the area vary over more than two dozen types, for the most part acidic and minimally fertile. Underlying them are beds of firm to very firm clay, creating difficulties with drainage and foundation settling that plague homeowners and prospective developers to this day.

Nevertheless, the first human pioneers found a hardwood forest and ground enriched by centuries of autumn leaves. Those adventurers may have arrived as early as 12,000 B.C.E. In Carolina-to-be, these "paleo" and "archaic" Native Americans presumably gathered from the woods and harvested game such as bison, bear, and elk, which later arrivals would record with pen and paper.

By the time those of pen-and-paper persuasion arrived, the nomadic adventurers had taken up agriculture to supplement what they could gather and hunt, and settled down for the long term. A replica of one of these villages stands in an Eno riverside park in Hillsborough, a few miles upstream from Durham: a circular wall of upright poles enclosing a few wattle-and-daub huts. Tradition has graced the area with a number of "Indian burial grounds."

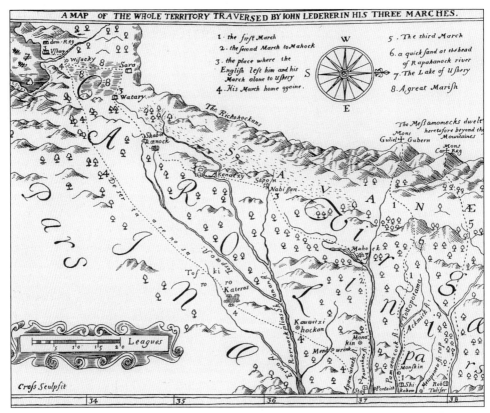

A 1672 MAP OF THE VIRGINIA AND CAROLINA INTERIOR. This map indicates the routes taken by John Lederer on his three 1670 expeditions for the governor of Virginia.

A PALISADED NATIVE AMERICAN TOWN. Theodore de Bry engraved this image of a town near the Ablemarle Sound. European explorers found similar settlements farther inland, some near present-day Durham. (Courtesy of North Carolina Division of Archives and History.)

Early pen-and-paper accounts suggest that migrations were still frequent, due to overpopulation and war—indeed, a state of war appears to have been constant (in good weather) between northern and southern nations along the Appalachian foothills from South Carolina to Pennsylvania. Near the future site of Durham, though, accounts record inhabitants as peaceable and industrious, with commercial contacts running far and wide: seventeenth-century explorer John Lederer took particular notice of small wheels used by the Oenock (Eno) people for keeping track of time, "because I have heard that the Mexicans use the same."

Lederer, a German physician, published the earliest written account of the Eno River area for *The Discoveries of John Lederer, In three several Marches from Virginia, to the West of Carolina, And other parts of the Continent, Begun in March 1669 and ended in September 1670.* Commissioned by Virginia Royal Governor William Berkeley "to go into those parts of the American Continent where Englishmen never had been"—as put by Lederer's editor Sir William Talbot, Baronet—Lederer was later forced to flee the colonists' outrage that his travels had been financed from the public purse.

Nevertheless, in the Virginia-Carolina piedmont, which Lederer called "highlands" and the Native Americans "Ahkontshuck," the explorer found thick and viny woods harboring "all sorts of beasts of prey," along with populated parts "pleasant and fruitful, because cleared of wood, and laid open to the sun."

In June 1670, traveling with a "Sasquesahanough-Indian" named Jackzetavon after being abandoned by his English companions, Lederer visited the Roanoke River island Akenatzy. The island afforded its numerous inhabitants, who led a communal existence under a pair of kings, a safe haven from warlike neighbors, but when the Akenatzys murdered a delegation from a neighbor tribe under a pretense of hospitality, "the bloody example . . . frightened me away."

From Akenatzy, Lederer headed south-southwest, "sometimes by a beaten path, and sometimes over hills and rocks," and in two days reached the Oenocks. He recorded his findings:

> Their town is built round a field, where in their sports they exercise with so much labour and violence, and in so great numbers, that I have seen the ground wet with the sweat that dropped from their bodies: their chief recreation is slinging of stones. They are of mean stature and courage, covetous and thievish, industrious to earn a peny; and therefore hire themselves out to their neighbours, who employ them as carryers or porters. They plant abundance of grain, reap three crops in a summer, and out of their granary supply all the adjacent parts. These and the mountain-Indians build not their houses of bark, but of watling and plaister. In summer, the heat of the weather makes them chuse to lie abroad in the night under thin arbours of wild palm. Some houses they have of reed and bark; they build them generally round: to each house belongs a little hovel made like an oven, where they lay up their corn and mast, and keep it dry. They parch their nuts and acorns over the fire, to take away their rank oyliness; which afterwards pressed, yeeld a milky liquor, and the acorns an amber-colour'd oyl. In these, mingled together, they dip their cakes at great entertainments and so serve them up to their guests as an extraordinary dainty. Their government is democratick; and the sentences of their old men are received as laws, or rather oracles, by them.

From the Oenocks, Lederer went 14 miles southwest to the Shackory, who dwelt "upon a rich soyl"—probably in the area between the Eno and Haw rivers shown on later maps as the Haw Old Fields—and whose customs and manners were so much like those of the Oenocks that Lederer pressed on to parts unknown. Before returning to Virginia, his second march would reach as far west as the Sauratown Mountains, above present Winston-Salem, and south beyond "Wisacky," perhaps the present Waxhaws district near Charlotte and Rock Hill, South Carolina.

After Lederer, it was 31 years until another pen-and-paper chap came Eno way. Other cryptic references, inferences from other sources, and informed conjecture suggest regular contact between the earlier residents and newcomers from parts elsewhere (a pattern and a dynamic of new arrivals meeting old-timers that continues to this day), beyond the scope and sight of colonial authority.

HISTORIAN TOM MAGNUSON, FOUNDER OF THE TRADING PATH PRESERVATION ASSOCIATION. *Here, he is walking a portion of the old roadway west of Durham. Centuries of commerce by foot, horse, then wagon created a ravine that survives, in places, more than 6 feet deep and 40 feet across.*

Governor Berkeley was moved to send Lederer after the Oenocks in particular, since one of his predecessors had described them as a "great nation" that had held back the encroaching Spaniards. A letter of 1673 recounts white traders visiting the Oenocks' town and employing a guide from the Occaneechee, Lederer's Akenatzy, who would leave their island and move south to the Eno after some unpleasantness during Bacon's Rebellion in 1676.

While colonialism came by way of the nature-favored harbors and rivers of Virginia and South Carolina, bypassing for the most part the sound- and shoal-guarded coastline in between, there is reason to assume intercontinental contact was taking other forms in the back country of North Carolina. (The Carolina colony was split into north and south divisions in 1710.) Legends of Native Americans with blue eyes and English names have been invoked for decades in fanciful accountings for the "lost" Roanoke Island colony of 1587. Shipwrecks along the stormy Outer Banks, where the cold Labrador Current hits the warm Gulf Stream, likely contributed survivors from faraway places to the native population, which further swelled with slaves, indentured servants, malcontents, and wanderlusting types escaping the colonial establishments.

Historian Tom Magnuson of Hillsborough, founder of the Trading Path Preservation Association, envisions central North Carolina from about 1600 to 1750 as home to a libertarian, live-and-let-live society in which Native American, Caucasian, and African American mixed. The three cultures lived in relative isolation, official anonymity, and social counterpoint shocking and disgraceful to any intruding representation of Anglican propriety. Indeed, in 1714, Virginia

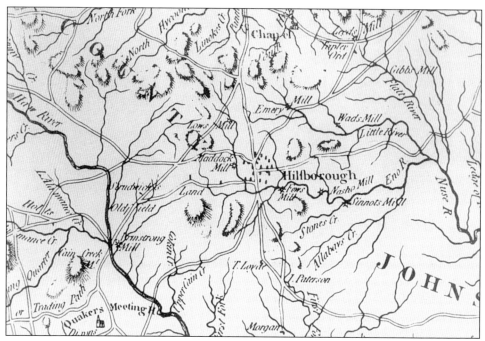

DETAIL FROM HENRY MOUSON'S MAP OF 1775. *This map depicts North and South Carolina, showing the colonial network around the Orange County seat of Hillsborough. The Trading Path is marked at the lower left.*

Governor Alexander Spotswood disparaged North Carolina as a place to which "loose and disorderly people daily flock."

Such an impression is further recorded by the Virginian William Byrd II, who was born in 1674, tutored on the Continent, instructed in law in London, speculated in land, expanded his inherited fortune, and, being a loyal public servant of crown and colony, was appointed in 1728 to a commission surveying the boundary between Virginia and North Carolina.

Byrd's impressions of North Carolinians, recorded in his *History of the Dividing Line*, were not generally favorable. To begin with, the North Carolina commissioners arrived at the appointed starting point "better provided for the Belly than the Business," two of them late. The first Carolinians the surveyors met were a hermit and his "wanton Female," who resided in a bark bower, subsisted on oysters and milk appropriated from neighbors' cattle, and made themselves decent with no more covering than beard and hair. Byrd recounted some impressions:

> Thus did these Wretches live in a dirty State of Nature, and were mere Adamites, Innocence only excepted.
>
> We came upon a Family of Mulattoes, that call'd themselves free, tho' by the Shyness of the Master of the House, who took care to keep least

in Sight, their Freedom seem'd a little Doubtful. It is certain many Slaves shelter themselves in this Obscure Part of the World, nor will any of their righteous Neighbours discover them. On the Contrary, they find their Account in Settling such Fugitives on some out-of-the-way-corner of their Land. . . .

Nor were these worthy Borderers content to Shelter Runaway Slaves, but Debtors and Criminals have often met with the like Indulgence.

At this point, Byrd is describing the northeastern region above the Albemarle Sound closest to the well-ordered Tidewater Virginia. One may reasonably assume he would have found affairs even less to his liking had he ventured deeper into the Carolina wilds. Three weeks into the expedition, nearing the substantial town of Edenton, North Carolina, Byrd summarized:

Surely there is no place in the World where the Inhabitants live with less Labour than in N. Carolina. It approaches nearer to the Description of Lubberland than any other, by the great felicity of the Climate, the easiness of raising Provisions, and the Slothfulness of the People . . . The Men, for their Parts, just like the Indians, impose all the Work upon the poor Women. They make their Wives rise out of their Beds early in the Morning, at the same time that they lye and Snore, till the Sun has run one third of his course . . .

Thus they loiter away their Lives, like Solomon's Sluggard, with the Arms across, and at the Winding up of the Year Scarcely have Bread to Eat.

To speak the Truth, tis a thorough Aversion to Labor that makes People file off to N. Carolina, where Plenty and a Warm Sun confirm them in their Disposition to Laziness for their whole Lives.

For their disinterest toward religion, Byrd would liken North Carolinians to "the Hottentots of the Cape of Good Hope;" for their shiftlessness, he would huff over the lack of quality standards for Carolina tobacco; and for their tendencies toward anarchy, he reported a magistrate who, so reckless as to order a drunk-and-disorderly fellow to the stocks, found himself taken there "and narrowly escap'd being whippt by the Rabble into the Bargain."

Going on west, the surveyors crossed the Trading Path at just about the point where Interstate 85 now crosses the state line, having just departed the last whites they would meet. Relying, no doubt, upon others' observation, Byrd wrote that the Path ran "thro' a fine Country, that is Water'd by Several beautiful Rivers. Those of the greatest Note are, first, Tar river, which is the upper Part of Pamptico [Pamlico], Flat river, Little river and Eno river, all three Branches of Neuse."

Among those others' observations, in all likelihood, were those of John Lawson. Lawson's origins have been a matter for scholarly speculation. He may have come from Scotland, Yorkshire, or London. By his own account, in the year 1700 he contracted an urge to travel and met a gentleman experienced of the world who "assur'd me, that *Carolina* was the best Country I could go to."

Arriving in August or September in Charles Town, South Carolina, Lawson somehow contrived an appointment to survey the colony's interior. On December 28, with a party of five other Englishmen and four Native Americans, he set out and, in 59 days, completed a 550-mile journey taking him past the future sites of Columbia, South Carolina, as well as Charlotte, Salisbury, Lexington, Swepsonville, Hillsborough, Durham, Goldsboro, Greenville, and Washington, North Carolina.

In his account of the expedition, *A New Voyage to Carolina,* published in London in 1709, Lawson echoed Lederer's favorable opinion of the "rich soyl" north of the Haw River—"rich Land enough to contain some Thousands of Families"— and described the interior as "the flower of Carolina." There, headed for *"Achonechy*-Town," he encountered great flocks of turkeys and a company of Virginia traders who advised him against following the Trading Path toward Virginia because of hostile Indians along the way. Rather, the traders suggested he head east toward Roanoke Island, near the white settlements above Albemarle Sound, and seek out for guidance a Native American named Enoe Will. Lawson and his companions were well received at Achonechy:

> The *Indians* presently brought us good fat Bear, and Venison, which was very acceptable at that time. Their Cabins were hung with a good sort of Tapestry, as fat Bear, and barbakued or dried Venison; no *Indians* having greater Plenty of Provisions than these. The Savages do, indeed, still possess the Flower of *Carolina*, the *English* enjoying only the Fag-end of that fine Country.

A couple of hours after their arrival, who should arrive but the aforementioned Enoe Will. Will, Lawson found, was of the Shoccori nation and "chief Man" of a mixed group of Shoccories, Enoes, and Adshusheers. Will agreed to conduct the explorers to English territory and the next morning they left the Virginia path and traveled east toward the Adshusheer village.

"It was a sad stony Way," Lawson wrote. They crossed a small stream at Achonechy, then proceeded for 14 miles, crossing several other streams, "which empty themselves in the Branches of *Cape-Fair.*" The route was so rocky that Lawson came up lame and lagged behind the others, but when he finally reached Will's house, he was treated to hot bread and bear oil.

Lawson describes Adshusheer only as being near a "pretty Rivulet" and "a prodigious overgrown Pine-Tree," the first timber of that sort he had seen for 125 miles. Conjecture has placed the town northwest of present Durham or northeast on the Flat River. However, planners of a 300th anniversary reenactment of Lawson's trek in February 2001, following clues in Lawson's text and on the present-day ground, put Adshusheer instead on New Hope Creek between Durham and Chapel Hill in the Hollow Rock area.

DETAIL FROM JOSHUA FRY AND PETER JEFFERSON'S MAP OF 1775. The map traces the Trading Path across the Flat, Little, and Eno Rivers and past the village Akonichi. Explorer John Lawson had spent a night there in 1701.

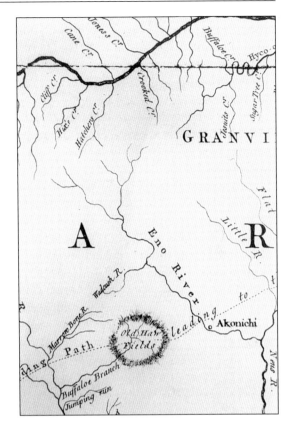

Such a location is further suggested by a tradition reported in the *Durham Morning Herald* of May 5, 1940, that a village of Eno Indians had stood on the west bank of New Hope Creek about 200 yards south of the Erwin Road bridge. When white settler John Patterson took title to the land in 1744, he found the group gone, but the ground still cleared and easily cultivated. When the creek overflowed, bones and relics were frequently left exposed from an old burial ground and on "The Field"—as the site was called—children played with rounded stones like those Lawson described the Indians using in a shuffleboard-like game called "chenco." Curtis Booker, a Patterson descendant who grew up nearby in the 1950s, recalls innumerable arrowheads, pottery shards, and even intact vessels recovered from the field and area nearby. Lawson recorded all that he saw at Adshusheer:

> Our Guide and Landlord *Enoe-Will* was of the best and most agreeable Temper that ever I met with in an *Indian,* being always ready to serve the *English,* not out of Gain, but real Affection. Which makes him apprehensive of being poison'd by some wicked *Indians,* and was therefore very earnest with me, to promise him to revenge his Death, if it should so happen. He brought some of his chief Men into his Cabin,

and 2 of them having a Drum, and a Rattle, sung by us, as we lay in Bed, and struck up their Musick to serenade and welcome us to their Town. And tho' at last, we fell asleep, yet they continu'd their Consort till Morning.

Lawson would go on to help establish North Carolina's first two English towns, Bath and New Bern, and to die at the hands of Tuscarora Indians in 1711. Will may have gone on, years later, to make the acquaintance of William Byrd. In Byrd's *Journey to the Land of Eden*—an account of visiting property he bought in North Carolina after the surveying was done—he recorded a "Shacco Will," who told him about a silver mine on the Eno River and, for his trouble, received a bottle of rum. "He made himself very happy," Byrd wrote, "and all the Familey very miserable by the horrible Noise he made all night."

Descendants of those indigenous residents remain in the area of Durham and Hillsborough, waging a long, drawn-out campaign for official recognition as Native Americans by the state of North Carolina. Traces of the old Trading Path remain, notably at the Ayr Mount historic site in Hillsborough, where a great gouge in the earth records the passage of trade wagons and stone foundations indicate the location of a wayside tavern.

EXPLORER JOHN LAWSON. He traveled near the future site of Durham in 1701 and met his end at the hands of hostile Tuscarora Indians in 1711. Lawson was captured on Contentnea Creek, a tributary of the Neuse River. (Courtesy of the Trading Path Preservation Association.)

Officialdom, of the sort that assigns titles to and assesses taxes upon land, arrived in the Carolina back country in the 1740s. One William Reeves acquired 400 acres in present Durham County at the junction of Ellerbee Creek with the Neuse River, in 1746. About the same time, several other individuals were recorded on the Flat and Little Rivers. By 1752, interior population had grown to the point that the colonial government, downstream in New Bern, created Orange County, covering the present territories of Orange, Alamance, Caswell, Chatham, and Durham Counties, plus bits of Guilford, Lee, Randolph, Rockingham, and Wake.

The western section of Orange County was settled largely by Pennsylvanians, crossing down the Shenandoah Valley and bringing with them the Lutheran and Quaker faiths still common in that region. The eastern section, which would become Durham County, was primarily settled by Virginians drifting down the Trading Path and some pioneers from older English settlements near the coast.

Among these immigrants came the family Few from Maryland. They arrived in Orange County in 1758, set their name upon Few's Ford on the Eno River, and gave posterity a description of the land in those days, as recalled by William Few, 10 years old at the time:

> There a new scene opened to us. We found a mild and healthy climate and fertile lands, but our establishment was in the woods, and our first employment was to cut down the timber and prepare the land for cultivation. My father had taken with him only four servants, who were set to work, and every exertion was made to prepare for the ensuing crop.
>
> Then it was that I commenced the occupation of a farmer. An axe was put into my hands, and I was introduced to a hickory tree about 12 or 15 inches in diameter, and was ordered to cut it down and cut off all the branches. There was novelty in the business which I was first pleased with, and cheerfully began the operation, but soon found myself extremely fatigued. My hands blistered, and the business progressed slowly. I thought my situation most deplorable, for I dared not to resist the order I had received to cut down the tree. I was obliged to proceed and found that practice every day made the labor more agreeable, and I was gradually instructed in the arts of agriculture; for that was all I had to learn. In that country, at that time, there were no schools, no churches, or parsons, or doctors, or lawyers; no stores, groceries or taverns, nor do I recollect to have seen during the first two years any officer, ecclesiastical, civil or military, except a justice of the peace, constable and two or three itinerant preachers. The justice took cognizance of their controversies to a small amount, and performed the sacredotal functions of uniting by matrimony. There were no poor laws nor paupers. Of the necessaries of life there were great plenty, but no luxuries. Those people had few wants, and fewer temptations to vice

than those who lived in more refined society, though ignorant. They were more virtuous and more happy.

Such a happy state could not last. Colonial administration in the back country proved oppressive and corrupt. In 1771, the Fews joined many of their neighbors in the Regulator uprising, smashed by Governor William Tryon and the provincial militia at the Battle of Alamance. William Few's brother James was hanged, the family farm was destroyed, and his father fled to Georgia. William joined the family there in 1776, going on to become a lawyer, a Continental officer, a politician, a delegate to the Constitutional Convention, a United States senator, and a federal judge before relocating and achieving more success in business and public service in New York.

For his trouble, Governor Tryon left the back country a military road that serves the population yet today, albeit under the name of a later colonial enforcer, Lord Cornwallis. As for the Fews, their lasting legacy to Durham was yet to come.

WILLIAM FEW. He fled North Carolina for Georgia after the 1771 Regulator uprising. There, he entered politics, was chosen a delegate to the Constitutional Convention, and elected one of his adopted state's first United States senators.

2. A Roaring Old Place

Soon after Trinity College moved from Randolph County, North Carolina, to Durham in 1892, there came to it a young scholar named John Spencer Bassett. Bassett was a graduate of the college, Class of 1888, who had taught two years in the Durham Graded School before earning his Ph.D. at Johns Hopkins and returning to Trinity as a professor of history in 1893.

Bassett had a literary bent, having been co-founding editor of the *Trinity Archive* magazine, and had an observant eye for society around him, as shown in his essay "Old Trinity Days," in which he noted that animosities between students of "upcountry" and "lowcountry" origin (Bassett was a lowcountry man himself, from eastern North Carolina) had been resolved by the unifying influence of intercollegiate baseball. Arriving back in Durham, he set about and encouraged others of the Trinity College Historical Society to collect oral history about the town. As a result, Bassett bestowed posterity with some of its few accounts of Durham's environs before there was a Durham. He wrote the following in his introduction to "Old Durham Traditions," published in the society's journal in 1906:

> Durham county is of recent origin, but the remarkably rapid development of its population, both as to numbers and as to changes in manner of living, serves to remove to a long distance from the present the customs and traditions of the region in the days when the county had not been thought of.
>
> Most of the people who remember the former days are now old, and it is but natural to expect that they will soon pass out of the world. It would, therefore, be proper if some one who has the true history of the community at heart would concern himself to gather up all the facts and interesting stories of the by-gone days and put them in printed and accessible form for the use and delectation of posterity.

The Trading Path was one of the traditions Bassett recounted. By the time of the Revolutionary War, advancing commerce and manners of transportation had transformed the "old pioneer's path" into a "great highway" entering northeastern

Durham County near the present crossroads of Hampton, passing near Willardville (at Staggsville and John Jones Roads) and running on, about 10 miles north of Durham, southwestward to Hillsborough.

"Will not some local antiquarian take upon himself the task of locating this old road exactly?" wrote Bassett. "And that done, will not some funds be raised for erecting memorials along its course by which men who pass may understand that this was the artery through which pulsated the first blood of civilization in these parts?" It would be 92 years before the formation of the Trading Path Preservation Association, but 11 state highway markers, more or less informative, would go up in 1941.

Bassett corrected one Durham tradition, that of crediting British General Cornwallis with building the road across southern Durham County, about 4 miles below town in 1906 that bears his name. Cornwallis Roads were common in central North Carolina, commemorating his army's 1781 route from Guilford Courthouse to Wilmington, and then north to final defeat at Yorktown, Virginia; however, going by Cornwallis's own descriptions of his route and that of his lieutenant Banastre Tarleton, Bassett concluded, "The British General never visited."

Cornwallis actually went farther south, after gracing Hillsborough with his presence for a few days. Upon inspection, Bassett concluded that Durham's

John Spencer Bassett. The Trinity College professor and his historically inclined colleagues recorded Durham tales and traditions soon after the school's move to town in 1892. (Courtesy of Duke University Archives.)

Cornwallis Road was indeed a product of British military engineering, "built after the ancient fashion which took no notice of grades," but gave credit to Tryon. "Till that time no good road had been made through the unsettled wilderness," Bassett wrote. "Only a bridle path marked the way and this was not practicable for artillery and the baggage wagons." So the royal governor had his militia blaze a trail adequate for his use, which he dubbed the "Ramsgate Road" for reasons of his own.

Not all Old Durham Traditions had to do with roads. Some others the Trinity historians found may have proved less useful to posterity but, now as then, rather more delectable. Take Pinhook, for example.

Before the Civil War, in the district that would one day be known as West Durham, downhill and south from the future Erwin Mills and the Blue Light drive-in and watering hole, there was a grove of trees and a well. Teamsters driving freight wagons along the Raleigh-Hillsborough road would stop off there to camp, sheltering in the woods and refreshing themselves from the well and a strategically located grog shop.

Where the name came from was not known, according to Bassett's associate W.S. Lockhart, who contributed to the "Old Durham" article. In later years, the term "pinhooking" would mean the underhanded practice of disguising inferior tobacco to get a better price at auction. Pinhook's heyday came long before a tobacco market opened in Durham, but perhaps the name then simply referred to the nefarious characters and disreputable behavior that gave Pinhook its reputation.

And a well-known reputation it was. Lockhart reported, "Its fame spread as far as 12 or 15 miles northwest, as may to this day be learned from the old inhabitants of the country communities." It spread that far southwest too, even to the groves of academe in Chapel Hill, whence young scholars would repair to Pinhook, seeking release from the pressure of their studies where they were safely out of sight of the University of North Carolina's faculty.

"It was known as a place of brawls and rough-and-tumble fights, drinking, gambling and other forms of amusement," Lockhart wrote, "where the natives and visitors met to have a rough, roaring, and, to them, glorious time." Pinhook, he found, was but the most renowned of "a number of houses of rather shady reputation" along the ridgeline that Durham would one day occupy. Collectively, they became known as "a roaring old place," an image that would endure well after more respectable industries arrived, and carries on to the present day.

The reputation and character of proto-Durham were the products of geography, Lockhart thought. Along the ridge, the soil was poor and unsuitable for cultivation. Sturdy yeomen who settled fertile grounds to north and south set about improving their land and making their homes. Folk of the sluggard sort drifted toward the high, but poor, ground in search of opportunity, or at least the company of their own kind.

"As we all know," Lockhart wrote, "the shiftless and poor are liable to give way to the less refined forms of vice. Also it is likely that the vicious element from

DOWNTOWN DURHAM, 1880s. Watering holes and their corollary carousing gave the ridge a "roaring" reputation that long predated formation of the town. (Courtesy of Durham County Public Library.)

adjacent sections drifted into such places as this, being spurned by the more wealthy communities."

In their own way, Lockhart's "shiftless" and "vicious" were simply Governor Spotswood's "loose and disorderly people," seeking elbow room and liberty from preachers, proprietors, and prying eyes. Their migration from communities north and south replicated, on a small scale, the earlier movement of runaways and malcontents out of colonized Virginia and into the Carolina wilds.

West from Pinhook, near today's intersection of Hillsborough and Morreene Roads and the Walden Pond apartments, there was a clear spring owned, around the 1830s, by a family named Peeler, "of poor social standing." They, too, profited from traffic along the Hillsborough-Raleigh road, selling spirits and keeping an inn where "uproarious times were often witnessed." There were two boys, with the local-colorful names of Pet-Tich-Eye and Red-Wine, and there was Old Ben Peeler, who often killed his lodgers, dumped their bodies in a well, and took their horses to sell in Raleigh. H.A. Neal, who lived near the spring and the decayed ruins of the inn (nearby Neal Road was named for his family), had collected the Peeler stories earlier and passed them along to Bassett.

In time, the North Carolina Railroad would transform life and commerce along the ridge, but the story of the railroad's arrival was preserved in a roaring old form. Intended to connect interior North Carolina with seaports at Wilmington and Beaufort, the railroad was laid out in an arc from Charlotte, in the west, to

Goldsboro, on the Neuse River to the east, and the north-south Wilmington and Weldon line. Construction went on from each end. When tracks got close, word came to the roaring old place that a train was coming and a crowd assembled at the railhead to see this newfangled thing.

Among the crowd was an old rowdy called Wash, "known far and wide for his boisterous carousing," and his wife. When the train was late, Wash developed a thirst and went, over his wife's objection and riding a blind horse, to get a drink. He returned with a gallon jug of liquor just as the train came into view. Mrs. Wash ran yelling toward her husband, the locomotive blew its whistle, the startled horse bucked, and Wash went tumbling off. He landed intact, but not so the jug.

"Glory to God!" his wife exclaimed. "Wash is safe and his jug of liquor's broke!"

"Old Durham Traditions" gave only passing mention to a saloon proprietor who would figure significantly in Durham's future. This proprietor's property lay about 2 miles east of Pinhook. Going by the North Carolina Railroad's survey map of 1850, it was around 500 feet north of the right of way, approximately where the Edgemont Elms apartments now stand at Lyon Street and Angier Avenue. This was Prattsburg and it was owned by one William Pratt.

The railroad map shows "Pratt's Store" on the north side of the Raleigh-Hillsborough road and three smaller buildings on the south. Pratt had bought property at a crossroads there in 1832 and, the next year, was indicted for "keeping a disorderly house for his own lucre and gain at unlawful times as well on Sundays as other days." At Pratt's establishment, the indictment continued, there congregated "evil disposed persons of evil name" for "conversation," as well as "drinking, tipling, playing at cards and other unlawful games, cursing, screaming, quarreling and otherwise misbehaving themselves."

Other than that, Pratt operated a cotton gin and general store and, reputation notwithstanding, became postmaster on January 23, 1836. According to the National Postal Museum of Washington, D.C., a post office in what is now Durham was established on November 29, 1827 and named "Herndon's" for Postmaster William R. Herndon. When Pratt took over, the name was changed to "Prattsburg."

Along the planned railroad, Pratt's village was halfway between the towns of Hillsborough and Morrisville, just where the railroad needed a fuel and water stop. Railroad agents approached Pratt about using his land for a station and track, but he set an absurdly high price. Legend has it that Pratt was afraid passing trains would scare his customers' horses and hurt his business.

No doubt, the legend of Pratt figures into that of Wash, thanks to the process of folk memory. In more concrete form, it figures into the railroad, which to this day follows an odd curve coming into Durham from the southeast—a curve laid out to keep distance from Pratt and his customers. The railroad agents went one landowner west and there the modern city began. There is more, however, in the legacy of William Pratt to the city that would not be Prattsburg: it is from his illegitimate son Thaddeus Redmond that we have our most vivid account of the man who did give Durham its name.

Prescience is sometimes ascribed to Dr. Bartlett Durham. For example, there is his tombstone in Durham's Maplewood Cemetery:

BARTLETT SNIPES DURHAM
1822–1858
FOUNDER, THE CITY OF DURHAM
COUNTRY PHYSICIAN AND PUBLIC-
SPIRITED CITIZEN WHO DONATED
LAND FOR A RAILROAD STATION AND
THEREBY BECAME FOUNDER OF A CITY

"THE MERIT BELONGS TO THE BEGINNER SHOULD
HIS SUCCESSOR DO EVEN BETTER"

The year of Durham's birth, the year of his death, and his middle name are wrong, too. Bartlett Durham was born in 1824 and died in 1859, his middle name was Leonidas, and calling him the "founder" is a case of "for want of a better word." A founder, however, must have done something to deserve the honor of being thus named and so a Dr. Durham was concocted of hindsight, and the proprieties of an era passed that made the famous dead into civic models no matter what they had been in life.

In life, indeed, Bartlett Leonidas Durham was a country physician. He was born on November 3, 1824 about 12 miles west of Chapel Hill, son of William L. and Mary Snipes Durham, and fourth generation of his father's family in Orange County. As a young man, he studied medicine. He may have taken classes, as lore has it, at the University of Pennsylvania, though there is no record of his enrollment: most of his education he must have received "reading medicine" under the tutelage of a local doctor.

In 1847 or 1848, he bought 100 acres in the vicinity of the present Durham Bulls Athletic Park and the old American Tobacco factory, bordered by the properties of William Pratt on the east, John Turner on the west, and Andrew Turner on the north. Choosing that spot to hang out his shingle, Durham likely figured a situation between two such rowdy points as Pinhook and Prattsburg would assure his practice a steady stream of trade. He likely saw more opportunity knocking when the railroad men came to call, and so gave them 4 acres of his land.

Apparently, medicine was not enough to sustain a young fellow's needs and appetites. The town of Durham's first historian, Hiram Paul, wrote in 1884 that Dr. Durham became the railroad's station agent and was a partner in the first store to open in the depot's vicinity. (While Pratt remained postmaster, the office's name was changed to "Durham's" on April 26, 1853, about a year before the first train arrived, and presumably moved from Prattsburg to Durham's store, at the present corner of Main and Mangum Streets.) At their store, Durham and his partners John W. Carr of Chapel Hill, James Mathews, and M.A. Angier, were licensed to sell spiritous liquors. Notwithstanding that, as a country representative

BARTLETT DURHAM. He was a lover of good times, a businessman, politician, and physician devoted to his patients. If one died, according to W.T. Redmond, Durham would spend days drowning his sorrows. (Courtesy of Duke Special Collections.)

in the state legislature, Durham had introduced a bill to incorporate a Sons of Temperance chapter.

Thaddeus Redmond, whose family name also belonged to the Redmond Grove in which Prattsburg was located, was a small boy in those days. By his own account, he was born June 12, 1843, about 7 miles west of Durham. Many years later, he set down some of his memories:

> I knew Dr. Bartlett Durham. He boarded at Andrew Turner's house and Andrew Turner's house is where the Liggett and Myers tobacco factory is now.
>
> Dr. Bartlett Durham was a fine, portly looking man. He was a jovial fellow. On moonshiny nights he would get a group of boys together and serenade the town.
>
> In those days there were about a dozen families. I remember on one occasion Ed Lyon, L. Turner, Jim Redmond and Dr. Durham went out to serenade. I don't remember where we went. We had some horns, a fiddle and a banjo. We went by a barroom and got some liquor. Dr. Durham would go on a spree and when he did he would get into a fight. He would fight only when it was necessary, as he proved on one

31

occasion. Dr. Durham weighed about 200 pounds. He came in late one night. He knew Andrew Turner had a dog. On that occasion he was in the yard and the dog came towards him, the dog not having a [restraining] block on him. Dr. Durham got the dog in the collar and mastered him and sat down on him. There was great deal of talk at the time of how the doctor mastered the dog.

Dr. Durham never got married. He knocked around with the women a great deal, and he died at a woman's house by the name of Dollarhite. I have heard that they put him in an iron coffin. I do not know where they got it. There was a family of Pattersons that lived near New Hope Church who were very wealthy, and had three mills, Negro slaves and farms. One of the Pattersons had an iron coffin made for himself. It may be that Dr. Durham's coffin was made there. In those days they made liquor and drank liquor.

Dr. Durham was a fine man and when he was sober he was strong and courageous. Everybody liked him. We never heard anyone speak ill of him. He had a habit that when he had a patient and he was so sick that he lost hope of the patient getting well and he had done all he could for him, Dr. Durham would then go off and get on a spree. Sometimes it

THADDEUS REDMOND. Late in his life, Gettysburg veteran W.T. Redmond shared his boyhood memories of Dr. Bartlett Durham, who gave land to the railroad and a name to a city. (Courtesy of the Durham County Public Library.)

would be nearly a week or 10 days before any of his friends would see or hear of him.

In those days doctors carried their medicine with them and Dr. Durham would leave the medicine for his patient with instructions as to how to use it. When I was sick with typhoid fever and he attended me he went off and stayed several days. I was sitting in the lap of a neighbor who was at our house and Durham came by to see me. He stated that when he went away he did not expect to see me again.

That time at least, the good doctor was wrong about his patient. Redmond lived to the respectably old age of 92.

A different bit of local lore places Durham's residence in a house called Pandora's Box, in the block between Corcoran and Mangum Streets on the north side of the railroad, across from the depot. The railroad survey map shows a tavern near that location, with a few other unidentified buildings nearby, and Andrew Turner's residence a bit to the west and just over the line separating his property from Durham's. Perhaps the doctor lived in different places at different times. In any case, the intersection of Corcoran Street and the railroad, a block downslope from the ridgecrest and the Raleigh-Hillsborough road, is the point of Durham's beginning and the point from which its later fortune sprang.

But that gets ahead of our story. Bartlett Durham died of pneumonia at 34 years of age on February 2, 1859. His body was frozen by the time it reached its resting place in the Snipes family plot (his mother's people, undoubtedly the source of his much-repeated incorrect middle name) near Antioch Church, having traveled through a snowstorm and freezing weather and lain in state overnight at a Chapel Hill hotel.

By that time, some things had begun to develop around Durham's Station. As old-timers could recall it in the 1920s, there were, besides Durham's store, two other mercantile establishments up the hill from the tracks, a carpenter shop, two bars, a dozen or so residences, and a log school. A Masonic Lodge had been organized, as well as the Rose of Sharon Baptist Church, which, ironically enough, fulfilled the fears of saloon-keeper Pratt.

Organized before 1850, the church stood south of the railroad and very close to the tracks, such that the noise of passing trains regularly disrupted worship and spooked the horses hitched outside. Before long, the congregation pulled up stakes and moved north to the far side of the ridge, still the site of Durham's First Baptist Church. J.W. Cheek, one of the merchants of Durham's Station, took the old church building for his residence.

There was also a small house just west of the depot, where the partnership of Robert F. Morris and W.A. Wright had begun the manufacture of smoking tobacco.

The piedmont tobacco business had come a ways since Stephen's accidental discovery 20 years before. Abisha Slade, Stephen's owner, had made himself a veritable evangelist for charcoal curing—then as now, the boss receiving credit for

AN ELDERLY WASHINGTON DUKE. Duke is visiting one of his original tobacco "factories," a grandiose term for the sheds and shacks where early manufacturers labored by hand. (Courtesy of Duke Homestead State Historic Site.)

subordinates' good work—and as growers took up and refined his techniques, production of brightleaf tobacco spread through south-central Virginia and north-central North Carolina.

Contrary to what may be a logical assumption, the tobacco that made Southern fortunes is not the native leaf the Native Americans enjoyed. North American Nicotiana rustica produced a smoke too harsh for European taste, already conditioned to the milder Nicotiana tabacum grown in the Spanish Caribbean, by the time England's Jamestown colony became desperate for a product it could sell. From the 1610s on, North American producers sought to develop ever milder, smoother, and yellower tobaccos as their customers became ever more discriminating.

Soils along the Virginia–North Carolina border, between the coastal plain and the mountains, vary greatly from place to place. Some are well suited for yellow tobacco, a most finicky crop, some not so. Stephen's discovery and Slade's promotion helped farmers produce a relatively reliable, uniform leaf, pleasing on the palate. In turn, its culture helped relieve a condition of poverty general in the region and reverse a long trend of out-migration. The marketing of brightleaf tobacco, however, was limited by available transportation and, before long, by the War between the States.

Morris and Wright opened their tobacco factory in 1858. "Factory" is a grandiose term for their operation, which basically consisted of thrashing dried and cured tobacco leaves into tiny shreds that could be packed and smoked in a pipe, perhaps adding a little flavoring of one kind or another before putting it out for sale under a brand name. In the case of Morris and Wright, the brand name was "Best Flavored Spanish Smoking Tobacco."

Wright struck out on his own in 1861 and, the next year, Morris sold the business to John Ruffin Green, who had moved into town from his family farm on the Eno River. Green was a man of inspiration, his first being to go after the sophisticated smokers at the university in Chapel Hill for whom Durham's Station was the closest connection to the outside world. His product positioning worked, and thus the good word on Durham tobacco began going places.

JOHN R. GREEN. He thought he was ruined when soldiers raided his tobacco warehouse in 1865. Instead, they brought fortunes to him and the village of Durham's Station. (Courtesy of Duke Homestead State Historic Site.)

3. EVANGELISTS AND ENTREPRENEURS

John A. McMannen was a Virginian by birth, a preacher by call, and a visionary by gift from above and, we may reasonably assume, by adult inclination. Born to John and Hannah Duncan McMannen in Petersburg on June 4, 1812, young John moved south with his family, down the old Trading Path now become a wagon road, when he was about 10 years old.

The McMannens settled near the Little River in northeastern Orange County. McMannen took up his father's trade of coopering, turning out barrels and kegs for the farming neighborhood. A gifted fiddler besides, he would pass his talent and taste for music along into a family tradition, occasionally teaming with his children in a three-fiddle-and-piano combo. He also became a lay preacher of the Methodist persuasion, perhaps inspired by the itinerant evangelists who frequented the district in the fevers of the Second Great Awakening, leaving fledgling congregations along their circuits and, from time to time, returning to keep up the faith.

In contrast with the decorous service of the Church of England (from which many settlers came to North Carolina to get away) and the terror-inducing, "Sinners in the Hand of an Angry God" Calvinism of the eighteenth-century Great Awakening, the faith of the "Fiddling Preacher" stressed the experience of salvation, or "conversion." Conversion experiences, which not coincidentally helped to civilize the hard-drinking, eye-gouging, name-of-the-Lord-in-vain-taking American frontier, were commonly stimulated by ecstatic revivals and camp meetings, which could be just as emotional and indecorous as the back country's secular diversions.

A glimpse is afforded by the satirist Johnson Jones Hooper, North Carolina–born and removed to Alabama, through a misadventure of his fictional character Captain Simon Suggs:

> The excitement was intense. Men and women rolled about on the ground, or lay sobbing and shouting in promiscuous heaps. More than all, the negroes sang and screamed and prayed. Several, under the influence of what is technically called "the jerks," were plunging and pitching about with convulsive energy . . . "Keep the thing warm!"

roared a sensual seeming man, of stout mould and florid countenance, who was exhorting among a bevy of young women, upon whom he was lavishing caresses.

Revival religion, spreading along the Appalachian frontier from North Carolina to Ohio and among the yeoman folk at lower elevations, further contrasted with the Enlightenment skepticism common among the planter gentry. In 1829, Dr. Thomas Cooper, president of South Carolina College, described "the land & people" among whom he worked as "theologically ignorant and bigotted." Five years later, he was forced to resign in the wake of legislative charges that he was corrupting the young, "by sneers and insinuations attempting to bring into contempt Christianity as taught by the sects most prevalent in this state."

Bare-knuckle evangelism brought scriptural literalism and ready condemnation of such pleasures of the flesh—drinking, dancing, gambling, cussing, ignoring the Sabbath, and sex without benefit of clergy—as frequently led to or presaged fights, brawls, killings, and other breaks in the agricultural monotony. It became pervasive in the South and so remains. It may be fairly said that deep down in most Southerners, no matter how high-church, there is a Baptist.

In the early 1800s, though, Methodism was the evangelical variety that most took root in eastern Orange County. Its initial planting had been fertilized by the

THE "FIDDLING PREACHER." This picture depicts John A. McMannen in circuit-riding pose. (Courtesy of Mary-Jo Hall.)

July to August 1780 visit of the renowned minister Francis Asbury. He preached to a gathering he estimated at 400 at "Neuse meeting house," near the present Cheek Road bridge over Falls Lake; to "a settlement of Irish Pennsylvanians" at a place he called "Clenny's," probably the later Hardscrabble Plantation on St. Mary's Road; and at a Mr. Corney's tavern in Hillsborough, where the people "were decent, and behaved well." The subsequent Great Revival movement swept into Orange County in 1801, ecumenical at first, but increasingly favoring the Methodists with their theology of experiential conversion.

Such was the temperament of time and place that shaped the Fiddling Preacher and gave him his first vision in 1843. It was a vision of sin and salvation, a vision both evangelical and entrepreneurial. It was *The Christian Monitor: A Pictorial Representation of Life and Death*, engraved, printed, and suitable for framing.

McMannen engaged an artist, who produced an image contrasting sin and salvation. Across the bottom, three drawings of Christ captioned the following: "He rose for our justification," "He died for our sins," and "He hath ascended up on high." At the top, a virtuous Christian risen to reward in the presence of angels. To the sides, a dark and angry storm whirls "Uneasiness of mind," "Love of money," "Sabbath breaking," "Self-esteem," and so forth about a central pillar of calm, tagged "In heaven is our eternal life," "The last battle fought," "Temperate in all things," "Industry, perseverance, economy," and so on. To either side, the

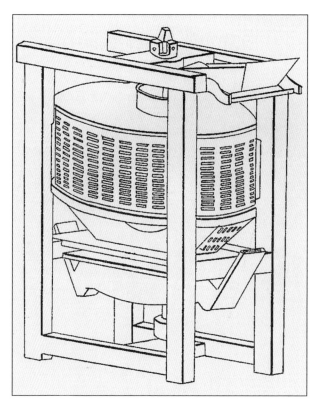

DETAIL OF A SMUT MACHINE. This portion of a patent diagram shows what John McMannen was manufacturing at South Lowell. (Courtesy of Ed Clayton and Mary-Jo Hall.)

lament, "O Eternity, Eternity, Eternity!" and, running down the edges, a sermon on "Sinner's Doom."

The print was issued in paper and satin editions, with mahogany and gilt frames, respectively. It was a hit. Orders rolled in. Visionary that he was, McMannen took his profits and invested in the business of smut.

Smut, that is, of the fungal sort that attacks cereal grains such as wheat, which was, along with corn, the area's principal crop. McMannen bought a patent on a "smut and screening machine," which separated diseased from wholesome wheat as the grains were ground. He set up to manufacture the gadgets at John Leather's gristmill on the Little River's North Fork and, again, made a killing so impressive and inspiring that the community around his smut works became known as "South Lowell" in emulation of the Massachusetts town then booming with cotton mills.

McMannen bought out the mill and property nearby and built an imposing home on a crest overlooking his mill for his family of 10 children. South Lowell grew, with a post office, male and female academies, and such cultural amenities as a debating club and a temperance society. Sometimes, the McMannen family musicians would play for their neighbors, as recorded by South Lowell Academy student James Gill: "Mr. Mc and two of his sons are fiddlers. They play with the piano and it makes very nice music." With his other pursuits, McMannen carried on with his saddlebag ministry, preaching under trees and brush arbors, marrying and burying, and helping new congregations get together.

Orange County in those days was a country of rural "neighborhoods," according to studies by Brigham Young University historian Robert Kenzer. They were, to a large degree, self-enclosed and isolated from the neighborhoods around them, defined by kinship and marriage relations, and made stable by the ties that bind. Their country churches were a broadening of the extended families that made up their congregations, soothing over family grudges and promoting a common set of values.

Such ties proved strong enough to keep neighborhoods intact, even through the out-migration in North Carolina's depressed "Rip Van Winkle" era up to the 1840s. While agricultural wealth streamed out to markets in Virginia and South Carolina and a conservative, tax-opposing state government, dominated by eastern planter interests, blocked internal improvements such as roads and canals, North Carolinians pulled up stakes and headed west. Some Orange County households joined the diaspora: many others—or elements of them—remained, such that upon the county's rolls are names appearing there since colonial times.

Adolphus W. Mangum, a student at the South Lowell Male Academy, who later became a minister and professor at the University of North Carolina, left a record of the time and place. His diary reflects a sense of continuity in his native Flat River neighborhood:

> I crossed the fence below the old schoolhouse spring & here . . . were
> the trees that I used to climb with my supposed agility, the old spring

ENO RIVER FLOOD SOAKING CHRISTIAN'S MILL, 1908. Necessarily located down by the riversides, gristmills were often victims of high water. (Courtesy of West Point on the Eno Park.)

around which we used to meet & indulge in mirthful glee. So pleasant were the hours that I spent there that I never shall forget the spot while I walk these mortal shores.

Besides the churches, general stores were gathering places to swap gossip and catch the news. Many of the stores took advantage of preexisting traffic, locating near stream fords and gristmills—sometimes as adjunct enterprises to the mills, which were in business by the 1750s in eastern Orange County.

The first record of these appears in a land grant of 1752 to one Michael Synott, describing 100 acres of land on the Eno River, "including his mills," indicating he was already grinding away. Synott also ran a tavern where, among others, he sheltered the Moravian Bishop Spangenberg on his way to visit the sect's settlement at Bethabara, now part of Winston-Salem.

Legend has conveyed a miserly image of Synott, a bachelor sharp in real estate and well acquainted with the colonial courts. According to one old tale, he drowned in the Eno—at the supposedly bottomless Sennett Hole—during a flood that also carried away his mill and a pot of his hoarded gold and silver.

In time, as many as 30 mills would be in operation on the Eno River, itself only about 35 miles long, and more on the Flat and Little Rivers and on New Hope Creek in the south. Mills, stores, churches and, in time, post offices served as focal points for early villages like South Lowell. Others, in the St. Mary's tax district of northeastern Orange County, included Red Mountain (now Rougemont), Round Hill (Bahama), and West Point (site of the present West Point on the Eno city park). In the southern St. Mark's district, there was a community called Brassfield, but little else in a region of relatively poor soil, wetlands, and little settlement. According to the 1790 census, St. Mark's had 117 white taxpayers between 21 and 60 years of age: 44 of them owned 111 slaves aged 12 to 45. At the same time, St. Mary's had 218 taxpayers: among them, 58 owned 164 slaves.

One reason for the apparent statistical skew, identified by Durham historian Jean Anderson, is that the St. Mary's district—in marked contrast with the small farms and rural neighborhoods that characterized most of early-American and antebellum Orange County—included the extensive estates of William Cain, John Carrington Jr., and Richard Bennehan, who provided the county with what little it had in the way of the stereotypical Southern plantation. Across the county, the average land holding was just under 400 acres. Bennehan, however, owned 2,355 acres in 1790, while Carrington had more than 5,200.

The Carrington estate would decline from divided bequesting and financial reverses, but Bennehan's would dramatically grow. Another native of Petersburg, Virginia, Richard Bennehan came south in 1768 to become a business partner with the merchant William Johnston, whose earlier investments had included one of Daniel Boone's expeditions to Kentucky. He was quite successful running a store where the old Trading Path crossed the Little River, and bought land with his earnings. In 1787, he bought 66 acres from widow Judith Stagg whose husband Thomas had run a tavern that gave its name to the place: "Stagville."

That same year, Bennehan built a home for himself and his family at Stagville, modest at about 600 square feet, but one that would receive most of North Carolina's important people, such as William Hooper, a signer of the Declaration of Independence; James Iredell, a justice of the United States Supreme Court; and William Davie, primary motivator behind creation of the state university.

Bennehan himself was an early University of North Carolina trustee and man of means. By 1800, he had acquired 4,000 acres and 40 slaves, plus an addition onto his home, though it remained small, utilitarian, and rustic, a far cry from the Tara that modern visitors often arrive expecting. In keeping with the family's stature, Bennehan's daughter Rebecca married a judge and politician of the county seat, Duncan Cameron. In 1810, he began building a new big house, Fairntosh, a few miles west of his father-in-law.

Fairntosh made a statement, according to Kenneth McFarland, a former manager of the Stagville state historic property: " 'We are in the process of becoming the richest family in North Carolina.' Which they did."

Under the care of Duncan Cameron and later his son Paul, Stagville/Fairntosh continued to grow and prosper. By 1860, the family owned 30,000 acres, about 900 slaves, various shops, stores, and mills, and more estates in Alabama and Mississippi. Their wealth and sense of mastery is attested by the plantation's Great Barn, a massive, slave-built structure 135 feet long, 33 feet wide, and 35 feet high at the center. Upon entering, a visitor has the impression of being in a cathedral. In 1860, the Camerons built with long-term expectations, as if it never entered their minds that the world they had helped build was about to be taken apart.

Richard Bennehan's son Thomas continued living in the old homeplace until his death in 1847. One of his best friends was his farm manager Fendal Southerland, an Orange County native born on February 22, 1800 along Ellerbee Creek, an Eno tributary that meanders across the northern part of present-day Durham. Southerland worked at Stagville for 25 years and the two men became close enough that Bennehan wrote a bequest for Southerland into his will.

In 1850, Southerland's health took a turn for the worse. He retired from Stagville and was succeeded by his brother Philip. Apparently, Fendal Southerland's condition improved, for in 1857 he used Bennehan's bequest to buy 1,435 acres on an island of high, sandy ground in southern Orange County between the marshy bottoms of Booker, Little, and New Hope Creeks. Southerland's was one of eight plantations along the sandy island where the peculiar soil was well suited for cotton cultivation.

In three years, Southerland became the third-leading cotton producer in Orange County, behind Paul Cameron and Cameron's neighbor on the Little River, John Lipscomb. He lived alone with 32 slaves, his only child Jane having married and moved to Chapel Hill. He built a cotton gin and a monumental barn of his own—also still standing, on Farrington Road—which housed a cotton press to pack the ginned fibers into bales for shipment. The press structure is long

RICHARD STANFORD LEIGH. He was a master of a 980-acre plantation on the sandy ridge between Durham's Station and Chapel Hill. (Courtesy of Curtis Booker.)

SLAVE CABIN AT LEIGH FARM IN SOUTHWESTERN DURHAM COUNTY. Richard Stanford Leigh owned 14 slaves. He also fathered 20 children by 2 wives, and his descendants are found in 1,000 present-day households in and around Durham.

disintegrated, but one component, a cog wheel 15 feet in diameter, survives to give an idea of the scale of Southerland's operation and the Old South's great expectations.

Southerland's neighbors on the sandy island included some of the oldest families of the county and the neighborhood: the Pattersons, Barbees, Morgans, and, later arriving, the Markhams and Leighs. Richard Stanford Leigh, Southerland's neighbor just to the north, was in his family's third generation in Orange County, his grandfather John having settled there about 1784. He received 500 acres as a wedding present from his father and grew his holding to 980 acres and 16 slaves by the time of the Civil War. He also produced 20 children (by two wives) and 89 grandchildren: by the 1990s, approximately 1,000 Durham-area households could trace their lineage directly to him.

Scattered about the county, there were a few free African Americans, their numbers slowly rising from 116 in 1800 to 528 in 1860. Census data shows that they lived among their white neighbors with no pattern of racial separation and both remained in the county over successive generations. Some African Americans were skilled artisans: one, Thomas Harris, was a lawyer. Most were small farmers and indications are that they traded, gossiped, and even worshipped alongside their white counterparts, although their liberties were legally restricted in response to the Nat Turner insurrection in Virginia in 1831.

Nonetheless, Orange County's 5,108 slaves dwarfed the free blacks' numbers at the verge of the Civil War. Even before Turner's rising spread terror among

Southern whites, including the 11,311 of Orange County, slaves lived severely circumscribed lives. In contrast with cinematic imagery, slaves were not strictly divided into field hands and house servants: many were, in fact, well-trained craftsmen who fashioned the metal, shod the horses, built the barns, and directed the labor vital to self-sufficient rural enterprises. Whatever their skill or status, however, their movements were limited, education (as distinguished from training) was discouraged if not forbidden, their initiative was controlled, and their lives were under constant scrutiny by owners, overseers, and court-appointed "patrollers."

Within those limits, there were exceptions and opportunities. Slaves might be sent on long-distance errands to sell crops or buy supplies, affording the chance to travel, share news, and extend a network of acquaintance. Skilled slaves might be hired out to other farms or businesses in town, on terms sometimes lasting years.

Living quarters on plantations were primitive, though often better than what freedmen were provided by Northern benefactors after Emancipation. Slaves, though, spent most of their free time outdoors, cooking, washing, tending personal vegetable plots, and sleeping, as long as weather was not too cold or wet. Their quarters became social replicas of African villages with cabins grouped around central common areas kept bare of grass to discourage insects and snakes, or in lines, with the space outside their front doors serving as Main Street.

Slaves' accommodations were similar on the small farms that were more typical of the South than plantations: there, however, the masters' quarters were barely, if any, different. Planters might never know their own slaves. Dr. James Cain from northern Orange County is recorded to have customarily stopped African Americans to ask, "Whose niggers are you?" If they were his, he would introduce himself. Yeoman families worked in the field and house right alongside their un-hired hands, eating the same plain food and wearing the same rough clothing.

Since slaves were expensive and valuable, owners generally provided well enough to keep their labor forces healthy and, if not content, resigned to life as defined by Master. Nevertheless, slaves were always and ever subject to brutalities and owners' whims. Interviewed in Durham when she was 85 years old, Sarah Debro recalled her youth under the Cain family for a Federal Writers' Project interviewer, whose rendition of her memories in dialect says far more about the social presumptions of the 1930s than it does about anyone's accent or syntax:

> Marse Cain was good to his niggers. He didn't whup dem like some owners did, but if dey done mean he sold 'em. Dey knew dis, so dey minded him. One day Grandpappy sassed Mis' Polly White [Polly White Cain, James's wife] and she told him dat if he didn't behave hisself dat she would put him in her pocket. Grandpappy was a big man and I ask him how Mis' Polly could do dat. He said she meant dat she would sell him, den put de money in her pocket. He never did sass Mis' Polly no more.

I was kept at de Big House to wait on Mis' Polly, to tote her baskets of keys and such as dat. Whenever she seed a child down in de quarters dat she wanted to raise by hand, she took dem up to de Big House and trained dem. I was to be a house maid. De day she took me my mammy cried 'cause she knew I would never be allowed to live at de cabin with her no more.

Even when an owner encouraged social conventions and family life among slaves, there were limits and higher priorities to be observed. Tempie Herndon, a slave of George and Betsy Snipes Herndon of Chatham County, recalled her wedding when she was interviewed in Durham at 103:

I married Exter Durham. He belonged to Marse Snipes Durham [no doubt a relative of Dr. Bartlett Durham] who had de plantation 'cross de county line in Orange County. We had a big weddin'. We was married on de front porch of de Big House. Marse George killed a shoat and Mis' Betsy had Georgianna, de cook, to bake a big weddin' cake all iced up white as snow with a bride and groom standin' in de middle holdin' hands. De table was set out in de yard under de trees, and you ain't never seed de like of eats. All de niggers come to de feast and Marse George had a dram for everybody.

Uncle Edmond Kirby married us. He was de nigger preacher dat preached at de plantation church. After Uncle Edmond said de last

STAGVILLE'S HORTON GROVE. This is one of the best-preserved examples of slave housing remaining in the United States.

words over me and Exter, Marse George got to have his little fun. He say, "Come on, Exter, you and Tempie got to jump over de broom stick backwards. You got to do dat to see which one gwine be boss of your household." Everybody come stand round to watch. Marse George hold de broom about a foot high off de floor. De one dat jump over it backwards, and never touch handle, gwine boss de house . . . I sailed right over dat broom stick same as a cricket. But when Exter jump he done had a big dram and his feets was so big and clumsy dat dey got all tangled up in dat broom and he fell headlong. Marse George he laugh and laugh, and told Exter he gwine be bossed 'twell he scared to speak lessen I told him to speak. After de weddin' we went down to de cabin Mis' Betsy done all dressed up, but Exter couldn't stay no longer den dat night 'cause he belonged to Marse Snipes Durham and he had to go back home. He left de next day for his plantation, but he come back every Saturday night and stay 'twell Sunday night.

We had 11 chillen . . . I was worth a heap to Marse George 'cause I had so many chillen.

There were, however, some instances of rough justice, such as this described by Lindsey Faucette of Durham, a former slave on the Occoneechee Plantation of Hillsborough attorney John Norwood:

TRYON MEETS THE REGULATORS. This after-the-fact sketch depicts the royal governor and his militia facing off with an unruly band of back-country folk during the 1771 uprising. (Courtesy North Carolina Collection at UNC, Bruce Cotten Collection.)

One time we had a white overseer and he whipped a field hand called Sam Norwood, till de blood come. He beat him so bad dat de other niggers had to take him down to de river and wash de blood off. When Marse come and found dat out he sent dat white man off and wouldn't let him stay on de plantation overnight. He just wouldn' have him round de place no longer. He made Uncle Whitted de overseer 'cause he was one of de oldest slaves he had.

Good, bad or indifferent, Norwood, Herndon, Durham, Cain—along with Lindsey Faucette, Tempie Herndon and Sarah Debro, Richard Stanford Leigh, and Fendal Southerland—would find themselves at the front line of a war.

War had brushed the future Durham two times in the past. The region was too far west to directly feel the effects of the Tuscarora War, downstream along the Neuse River, in 1711. Though its militia was called out for service, Orange County was too far east to feel the effects of the French and Indian and subsequent Cherokee Wars, which did send settlers nearer the mountains running for fortified sanctuaries.

Armed conflict arrived with the Regulator movement, which developed across the back country of both North and South Carolina in the 1760s. It was a movement to "regulate" colonial authorities who, settlers felt, were enforcing laws as suited them, pocketing tax money, extorting fees for legal services, and generally behaving as law above the law.

After appeals to the colonial assembly were ignored, Royal Governor William Tryon did receive a petition for redress of grievances and made some attempt to soothe their ruffled feelings, even traveling from New Bern to Hillsborough—no easy trip—to attend a session of court. Nevertheless, back country blood kept boiling and burst into a riot in Hillsborough in the fall of 1770.

With the Regulators talking more action and withholding tax payments through the following winter, the legislature passed a Riot Act and Tryon called up the home guard. In May 1771, he marched west, confronted a ragtag Regulator army near Alamance Creek, 25 miles west of Hillsborough, and promptly set it flying through the forest. One Regulator was hanged on the spot, six more after trials in Hillsborough, 6,000 laid down their weapons and agreed to be good subjects, while uncounted others kept going into the unregulated wilds of Tennessee and Georgia.

Just a few years later, the American Revolution came to central Carolina. Richard Bennehan was among the local citizens called to arms in 1776 to block a band of loyalist Scots who had immigrated to the Sandhills region near present Southern Pines and Pinehurst, after the Highlanders' destruction in 1746 at the Battle of Culloden. The Scots were headed to join the Redcoats at the coast. Bennehan never saw action, his unit being diverted to Cross Creek, present Fayetteville, rather than joining in the pivotal Battle of Moore's Creek Bridge near Wilmington. He had still left instructions for disposition of his property just in case, along with advice to keep a close eye on slaves, whom revolutionary talk might have infected with notions of liberty.

In 1781, the British army of Lord Cornwallis spent a few days at Hillsborough after its Pyrrhic victory at Guilford Courthouse. Some soldiers busied themselves by paving streets, at their commander's suggestion, while others relieved the area's homesteads of horses, food, whiskey, and anything else of interest not already liberated by foraging Continentals.

For, in truth, the American Revolution was a civil war, with the colonial population about equally split between rebellion and the status quo. In the back country, it was for the most part a guerilla war, if not a case of simple chaos with local authority weakened to the point that citizens were free to settle old scores and take advantages as they found them.

"It was a pretty unpleasant situation all the way around," said Kenneth McFarland, the former Stagville manager, a sentiment echoed by historian Lindley Butler:

> The Regulator movement had torn the colony apart just prior to the Revolution, so the whole back country was still distrustful of the provincial leadership, and they were the ones taking the colony into the Revolution. So they weren't interested in following people who were already oppressing them.

Ironically, settlers in the colonial interior saw the King and the royal governor as an audience willing to hear their complaints, while the provincial leaders, such as those in the assembly who had ignored them 10 years before, were perceived as the enemy. By the time Cornwallis passed through, the whole province of North Carolina had become Balkanized. Across the back country, homes and crops were burned, property was confiscated, and persons perceived as the wrong kind were jailed, killed, or harassed into flight.

The best known, or perhaps most infamous, figure of the Revolution in piedmont North Carolina was David Fanning, a Tory partisan from the Highland Scots so recently in arms against the English themselves. Early in the war, Fanning had been attacked by a gang of rebellious desperadoes and avenged himself for years with assassinations and organized attacks using his guerilla cavalry on rebel leaders, sympathizers, and supplies. Through three dozen actions throughout central North Carolina, he proved a reckless, bold, and daring leader.

In the summer of 1781, Fanning attacked and took Pittsboro, the seat of Chatham County immediately south of Orange, breaking up a session of court and taking officials prisoner. He then advanced on Hillsborough, where the state legislature was meeting, captured Governor Thomas Burke, and sent him off to British keeping in Charleston, South Carolina.

Fanning's were just a few of the atrocities committed by both sides, horrifying authorities who had to re-impose law and order after the war. Because guilt belonged on both sides, most bygones were left bygones and most perpetrators were pardoned. Citizens were willing to forgive and forget, since they knew investigations would bring to light their own crimes. Fanning, though, was one of

GOVERNOR THOMAS BURKE. Captured at his home near Hillsborough in a daring raid by Tory guerilla David Fanning in the summer of 1781, North Carolina's chief executive was packed off in chains to British-held Charleston. (Courtesy North Carolina Division of Archives and History.

three men declared outlaws in North Carolina, subject to being killed on the spot by anyone who might see him within the state.

Hindsight rendered the Revolutionary brutalities an embarrassment all around. They became something not spoken of in polite society and were obscured from historical memory by the events of 1861 to 1865.

"The truth would taint them all," said the historian Lindley Butler, who edited an edition of Fanning's journal. "And they ended up living side by side. They shook hands and went back to business."

Two generations later, business was going well in the part of Orange County that would become Durham. About 5 miles down the Little River from John McMannen's smut works at South Lowell, a pair of entrepreneurs brought industry to another gristmill village.

Partners John Douglas, son-in-law of the planter William Lipscomb, and John Webb, son of Hillsborough physician James Webb (under whom Bartlett Durham likely "read medicine"), went into the cotton thread and cloth business in 1852. They built their Orange Factory, a dam to power it, and four houses for millhands and their families. More labor commuted from the surrounding neighborhood. Their enterprise thrived and soon they built a new, larger plant, reaching more than 90 feet from its brick foundation to the peak of its roof, according to a workman on the job. The workman, one Thomas Dixon, also recorded a bad impression of his fellow builders: "Some to drink & all to sware, Fiddle & dance, play cards and so on."

By 1860, Orange Factory was turning out almost 150,000 pounds of cotton yarn and had a monthly payroll of $865 for 50, mostly female, hands. The partners also built a gristmill that ran off their factory dam and more worker shelter, including a 20-bed boarding house. A general store, school, and church appeared in due time and, in 1859, a post office. Webb was its postmaster.

Down on the Eno River, the Alpha Woolen Mills went into operation about the same time as Orange Factory. Gristmills kept grinding, cotton gins ginning, tanners and blacksmiths working away. Meanwhile, according to legend, Robert Webb, who owned a profitable window-shutter and -sash factory, was enticed to move his business south from Baltimore by the industrious John McMannen.

As for McMannen, ambition had outrun his abilities. Overextended by real estate speculation, McMannen declared bankruptcy in 1854. Barely fazed, however, and ever watchful for opportunity, the very next year he made a down payment on some land by a railroad stop and offered lots for sale. The May 26, 1855 issue of the *Hillsborough Recorder* newspaper advertised "Proposals for Building a Town:"

> The undersigned having purchased the property at Durham's Station, on the Great North Carolina Central Rail Road, is now making arrangements to lay off a town in half-acre lots, and proposes to give away, and make a full right and title to every other lot in the place, provided the individual who accepts the proposal will bind him or herself in a bond with good security, to build a certain class house on the same in the course of twelve months.
>
> The place is located in a fine, healthy section of the County, twenty-five miles west of Raleigh and twelve miles east of Hillsborough, and twelve miles north of Chapel Hill. Merchants and mechanics, and business men in general, will find this proposal worth their prompt attention.

McMannen was a visionary, but there were no takers for his proposals. The good Methodist had let his evangelical instincts outweigh his entrepreneurial ones and included in his terms of purchase a ban on the sale of booze.

4. BACKHAND BONANZA

One splendid April morning, a decade after John McMannen's abortive effort at building a town, the railroad that had brought Durham into being brought to the village a distinguished visitor.

It was April 17, Easter Monday of 1865, and the visitor was General William Tecumseh Sherman, USA, of incendiary fame. He arrived at Durham's Station in response to an overture from General Joseph Johnston, CSA, suggesting a cessation of hostilities so the generals might talk over the terms of peace.

Eight days earlier on Palm Sunday, Robert E. Lee had surrendered his personal command, the 28,231 men of the Confederate Army of Northern Virginia, at Appomattox Court House. While Lee's surrender was the seminal act in closing the War between the States—and the one that gets conventional credit—it was only the beginning of the end. Confederate forces remained in the field from North Carolina to Texas, 32,000 of them under Johnston's direct command.

For the past three months, Sherman's armies of Ohio, Georgia, and Tennessee had slogged north from Savannah, averaging 12 miles a day through a miserably wet winter across swamps, coastal plain, and, finally, the rolling red-clay Carolina uplands, moving toward an eventual link-up with Ulysses S. Grant's army besieging Richmond and Petersburg. Sherman's force of almost 89,000 had overcome Johnston's blocking attempt in the three-day Battle of Bentonville in late March, taken the railroad junction at Goldsboro, and there learned of Lee's surrender.

With the Confederate government in flight, but thousands of Rebels remaining under arms, Sherman advanced into Raleigh on Thursday, April 13. It was there, late the next evening, that he received an invitation to truce and negotiations— issued over Johnston's signature, but dictated in Greensboro by Confederate President Jefferson Davis. Sherman accepted the offer immediately, although his suspicious cavalry commander, Judson Kilpatrick, dithered and delayed before sending the message along to Johnston. Once Sherman's letter was received, subordinates arranged for the generals to meet on Monday morning along the road between Hillsborough and Durham's Station.

Sherman's memoir records that, as he boarded his train in Raleigh, he was handed an urgent telegram from Secretary of War Edwin Stanton, informing him

THE BENNETT FARM. Soldiers help themselves to farmer James Bennett's hay while their officers chat in the yard and the generals negotiate inside the house. (Courtesy of North Carolina Division of Archives and History.)

of Abraham Lincoln's murder on Friday night. Sherman ordered the telegraph operator to say nothing about it, pocketed the telegram, and set off for his rendezvous.

The train reached Durham at about 10 a.m. Sherman recorded only that he stopped into Kilpatrick's headquarters, then proceeded toward Hillsborough. Newspaper correspondents along for the ride recorded that it was a symbolically beautiful day, the air fresh after heavy rains and scented with pine, roses, and apple blossoms. Local residents, anxious for a view of the infamous Sherman, had packed into the old Rose of Sharon steeple beside the railroad, making the ironic impression that Durham's population was unusually pious.

Riding from their respective lines, Sherman and Johnston, with their escorts, met about 3.5 miles west of Durham's Station. After exchanging pleasantries, they retired to a roadside farmstead and, politely knocking, enquired of Mrs. James Bennett (at the time, spelled "Bennitt") if they might use her house for awhile. It is not likely that she would have refused, even without the presence of several hundred well-armed cavalrymen in her front yard. Mrs. Bennett and her family withdrew to an outbuilding, the generals went in to talk, and their escorts helped their horses to the Bennetts' store of feed.

With time out for consulting with superiors, Sherman and Johnston's negotiations and the associated cease-fire lasted nine days. During that time, wrote Hiram Paul, the first historian of Durham: " 'The boys in blue and gray' met in friendly intercourse—swapped horses, ran foot races, shot at targets and, around the same camp-fires, told hairbreadth escapes, spun camp yarns, and . . . around the camp-fires, in Durham, the 'blue and the gray' literally smoked the pipe of peace."

April 1865 has been called "The Month That Saved America." For certain, it was the month that made Durham.

As early as 1866, chroniclers of North Carolina's role in the War for Southern Independence began a tradition of emphasizing the Old North State's reluctance to enlist in the Confederate cause. In fact, North Carolina officials had attempted, in early 1861, to restrain other Southern states from rending the Union apart. Moreover, it was not until President Lincoln's call for North Carolina troops to help put down the insurrection, after South Carolina's attack upon Fort Sumter on April 12, that North Carolina aligned itself with most of the other slaveholding states. Its act of secession came May 20, timed to coincide with the anniversary of the Halifax Resolves of 1776, by which North Carolina delegates to the Continental Congress were directed to vote in favor of independence from Britain.

Cornelia Phillips Spencer of Chapel Hill, no friend to the Union cause, wrote about the events in her memoir *The Last Ninety Days of the War in North Carolina*:

> If it be true of the South in general, that even in the most excited localities warning voices were raised in vain, and that a strong

GENERALS JOHNSTON (LEFT) AND SHERMAN, 1865. *This magazine engraving depicts the generals talking inside the Bennett farmhouse.*

undercurrent of good sense and calm reflection undoubtedly existed—overborne for a time by the elements of strife and revolution—more especially and with tenfold emphasis is it true of the State of North-Carolina.

That North-Carolina accepted a destiny which she was unable to control, when she ranged herself in the war for Southern independence, is a fact which can not be disputed.

In his regimental history of the Sixth North Carolina Infantry, which included the Flat River Guards (Company B), the Durham Light Infantry (Company C), and the Cedar Fork Rifles (Company I) from eastern Orange County, Captain Neill Ray wrote:

> In the matter of secession, [North Carolinians] showed the same conservatism that characterized their deliberations whilst considering the Constitution before agreeing to become one of the United States. They cherished a hope for a pacific settlement of the questions then disturbing the country. When all overtures for peace had failed, Fort Sumter was bombarded and taken, and thereupon, the President of the United States called for troops to put down the rebellion—to coerce, to subjugate an independent State—then all the people, with few exceptions, manifested their willingness to resist any such attempt. North Carolina took her place promptly on the side of Constitutional rights and civil liberty, and most nobly did she maintain and hold her position to the bitter end.

Be that as it may, it had already been a year since the rising war fever reached eastern Orange County. R.F. Webb, captain of the Flat River Guards when they were absorbed into the Sixth Regiment, had organized the unit in February of 1860. W.K. Parrish, who would succeed Webb, was founding lieutenant. As the months went on, six more companies formed, including the Orange Light Artillery (Company G, 40th North Carolina) and Orange Cavalry (Company K, 41st).

Ray, a cadet at the North Carolina Military Institute in Charlotte when hostilities broke out, recalled early 1861 as "a time of great excitement—stirring events of great importance were following each other in rapid succession, and every mail was anxiously waited for."

Sarah Debro, Polly Cain's young housemaid, was caught up in the spirit of festivity:

> I was about waist high when de soldiers mustered. I went with Mis' Polly down to de musterin' field where dey was marchin'. I can see dey feets now when dey flung dem up and down, sayin', "Hep, hep, hep." When dey was all ready to go and fight, de women folk fixed a big

dinner. Aunt Charity and Pete cooked two or three days for Mis' Polly. De table was piled with chicken, ham, shoat, barbecue, young lamb, and all sorts of pies, cakes and things, but nobody eat nothin' much. Mis' Polly and de ladies got to cryin'. De vittles got cold. I was so sad dat I got over in de corner and cried too. De man folks all had on dey new soldier clothes, and dey didn't eat nothin' neither. Young Marse Jim went up and put his arm round Mis' Polly, his mammy, but dat made her cry harder. Marse Jim was a cavalry. He rode a big hoss, and my Uncle Dave went with him to de field as his bodyguard. He had a hoss, too, so if Marse Jim's hoss got shot dere would be another one for him to ride. Mis' Polly had another son, but he was too drunk to hold a gun. He stayed drunk.

Once committed, North Carolina responded to the Confederacy's call with apparent enthusiasm. The state contributed 125,000 men and 40,000 casualties to the war effort, more than any other seceding state and, thanks to the textile industry and massive effort on the home front, clothed and equipped its soldiers throughout the war. The war meant opportunity for Orange Factory, which got 75 percent of its work on government contracts, including cloth for Confederate uniforms. On the other hand, war put an end to the Alpha Woollen Mills when partners Charles Shields and Lorenzo Bennett (son of James Bennett, in whose home the generals did their talking) both died in Confederate service.

Wartime shortages and inflation made life hard for the women, children, slaves, and elderly at home. Cornelia Spencer recorded that even "families of the highest

ORANGE FACTORY ON THE LITTLE RIVER. This factory manufactured cotton cloth for Confederate uniforms. Built in the mid-1850s, the massive structure rose 90 feet from stone foundation to the peak of its roof. (Courtesy of Ed Clayton.)

respectability and refinement" made do with cornbread, peas, and sorghum molasses, that children went barefoot through winter and that carpets were made into blankets. Flour hit $800 a barrel, coffee went for $15 a pound. Even a plug of tobacco reached an astronomical $500. Word that a blockade runner had safely docked in Wilmington was cause for general rejoicing, for it meant there would be blankets, shoes, and medicine for sale. In the meantime, Spencer described how the boys in the trenches were in need as well:

> From the humble cabin on the hill-side, where the old brown spinning wheel and the rude loom were the only breastworks against starvation, up through all grades of life, there were none who did not feel a deep and tender, almost heart-breaking solicitude for our noble soldiers. For them the last barrel of flour was divided, the last luxury in homes that had once abounded was cheerfully surrendered.

Some of Orange County's noble soldiers were on hand for some of the Civil War's most dramatic moments. In its "baptism of blood"—as Neill Ray phrased it—at First Manassas, the Sixth North Carolina found itself engaged at the Henry House where their commander, Brigadier General Bernard Bee, "bravely calling on his men to stand firm against the heavy columns that were coming against

UNION GENERAL WILLIAM T. SHERMAN. He and his troops entered North Carolina on March 1, 1865 and, by April 17, he was at Durham's Station to talk surrender with Confederate General Joseph Johnston.

them, pointed down the line to General Jackson, saying, "Look at Jackson, he stands like a stone wall!"—words that will never die." The same could not be said for the outspoken Bee, who, shortly thereafter, took a fatal Yankee round.

Another casualty of Manassas was Lieutenant William P. Mangum, the son of former United States Senator Willie Mangum of the Flat River district, who had bid the Guards goodbye with the admonition, "You can't succeed. Their resources are too great for you." Before his death, young Mangum had complained of being tired to Major A.C. Avery, who recorded that Mangum thereupon "sat down beside or in the shadow of one of the deserted guns."

The Sixth would see more action on the Peninsula Campaign at Sharpsburg ("Antietam," in Yankee) and Fredericksburg in 1862, and at Gettysburg in 1863. There, in the ill-advised and worse-fated Pickett's Charge, the Sixth North Carolina established the Confederacy's "High-Water Mark" when it, along with a Louisiana unit, broke through the Union line and planted its colors on Cemetery Hill.

"We had full possession of East Cemetery Hill, the key to [Union commander George] Meade's position," wrote Ray, "and we held it for several minutes." That achievement was later immortalized in the state's unofficial motto: "First at Bethel, farthest at Gettysburg, last at Appomattox."

Thaddeus Redmond, the youngster treated and given up on by Dr. Durham, had grown up to join the Durham Light Infantry in May 1861 and was among the Confederates charging up Cemetery Hill. "They like to killed me there," Redmond said years later, and an arm wound suffered in the charge put an end to his military career.

For all the war's hardships, actual combat did not reach the vicinity of Durham's Station until almost the end. Anxiety, however, came ahead with Sherman's reputation. Cornelia Spencer wrote of early 1865:

> The tide of war was rolling in upon us. Hitherto our privations, heavily as they had borne upon domestic comfort, had been light in comparison with those of the people in the States actually invaded by the Federal armies; but now we were to be qualified to judge, by our own experience, how far their trials and losses had exceeded ours. What the fate of our pleasant towns and villages would be, we could easily read by the light of the blazing roof-trees that lit up the path of the advancing army.

Sherman's advance entered North Carolina on March 1, Ash Wednesday. Spencer, a Presbyterian, may not have noticed the ironic symbolism, but had she attended an Episcopal service that day, she would no doubt have been struck, if not shaken, had she heard the liturgical text from the prophet Joel:

> Let all the inhabitants of the land tremble: for the day of the Lord cometh, for it is nigh at hand; a day of darkness and of gloominess, a day

of clouds and of thick darkness, as the morning spread upon the mountains: a great people and a strong. A fire devoureth before them, and behind them a flame burneth: the land is as the garden of Eden before them, and behind them a desolate wilderness; yea, and nothing shall escape them.

Actually, by that time, the citizens of North Carolina had as much to worry about from their own side as from the Yankees. With local authority breaking down, the state government strained far beyond its resources, Confederate deserters and plain outlaws were making the most of reigning chaos while foragers from still-organized Southern units were making off with whatever remained to rural civilians.

As Sherman's main force settled into Raleigh on April 13, Kilpatrick's cavalry was hot in pursuit of retreating Rebs. A running battle developed, with firefights near the present Gardner and Pogue Streets in Raleigh and through what is now downtown Cary. At Morrisville, the Confederates under General Joe Wheeler stopped and built hasty fortifications around the railroad depot, where a train was taking on wounded soldiers and supplies for a run toward Johnston's receding line.

Reaching the ridge overlooking the Morrisville station, Kilpatrick brought up artillery and fired on the Rebel barricades, then sent 1,000 men charging. While townspeople took refuge in their cellars, the Confederates stalled the charge just long enough for the train to get away with the wounded, but the heavy supply cars were uncoupled for the sake of speed.

Making his headquarters at Morrisville, Kilpatrick split his force on the morning of April 14, sending one north up the railroad and the other west toward Chapel Hill. Meeting negligible resistance, the first wing advanced to Durham's Station. The second, though, was met with ferocity. The resulting carnage was such that, according to oral traditions in southern Durham County, at the end of the day, men could walk for yards on the bodies of dead horses.

Somewhere near the present-day line between southern Durham and northern Chatham County, 7 Confederates attacked a Federal patrol, killing 11 of its 12 men. The lone survivor, George Wolf, was offered a chance to surrender by an Alabama trooper named Eugene Dubois. Instead, Wolf shot Dubois dead and was immediately killed himself by Sergeant A.F. Hardee. Hardee found a slave nearby and told him to bury "the man in gray." The slave buried both men, one at each end of a fence.

Riding through the driving rain along the Chapel Hill Road—present Stagecoach Road—a detachment of Kilpatrick's Ninth Ohio reached New Hope Creek to find the smoldering remains of a bridge destroyed by retreating Confederates. Just as the Federals managed to ford the swollen creek, a Rebel charge swept down from the next ridge. One Southern rider shouted, "You drove us to Aiken," remembering an embarrassing encounter in South Carolina. "Now we're driving you!"

UNION CAVALRY COMMANDER JUDSON Kilpatrick. He used the Durham's Station home of Richard Blacknall for his headquarters and for keeping company with a woman Blacknall described as "vulgar, rude and indecent."

Fendal Southerland, the cotton planter on the sandy island, could have heard the fighting and seen flashes of gunfire from his front porch. The Confederates carried pistols and muzzle-loading, single-shot carbines. The Yankees had new Spencer repeating rifles. After four charges, three Rebels were dead and one wounded: the Federals had no casualties as the Confederates withdrew, leaving the Union soldiers to rebuild the bridge until a flood finally washed it out.

About a mile downstream, Union Colonel W.D. Hamilton sent four men to draw fire while the rest of his unit charged uphill against a Confederate artillery position. Abruptly, both sides ceased firing, word having reached them almost simultaneously that their commanders had called a truce.

In North Carolina, the last combat of the Civil War was over.

As had been the case all along Sherman's march in North Carolina—where Union officers had been ordered to restrain their troops' behavior in hopes of keeping the civilians civil—things remained fairly peaceable in the occupied towns, but not so in the country.

In announcing the ceasefire, Sherman admonished his soldiers: "The fame of this army for courage, industry and discipline is admitted all over the world. Then let each officer and man see that it is not stained by any act of vulgarity, rowdyism, and petty crime." Nevertheless, Yankee troops visited farms along the sandy island, requisitioning animals, food, and whatever else they fancied. Richard Stanford Leigh's plantation was relieved of all its livestock, most of its corn, and the contents of its smokehouse. After the war, Leigh filed a grievance and, in 1872, received partial compensation.

On the other side of the county, roving soldiers threatened to hang one landowner, while other citizens hid their molasses and their daughters. News of at least one rape reached Sherman's headquarters, eliciting a directive from aide L.M. Drayton to Kilpatrick: "Drum out the man who committed the rape of the negro woman and you will have the sanction of the general." Memories of stolen hogs, thieved chickens, and similar depredations would be passed on for generations.

The general, of course, had no control over the civilian "bummers" who tagged alongside his army, and little over straggling soldiers. Those elements were busily raiding on Easter afternoon, even as Sherman and Johnston prepared for their meeting and Northern cavalry made a quiet entry into Chapel Hill, where, Cornelia Spencer reported, "The silver had all been buried." At Fairntosh, the Cameron plantation home, drunken bummers went through the house and the slave cabins, taking clothes, bedding, vehicles, and ham.

Again, residents and their goods were attacked from both sides. According to local tradition, women raided supplies of meal at the West Point mill, where a crowd of undisciplined Rebel stragglers attracted the subduing establishment of a Federal cavalry post. The Yankees camped just uphill and east of West Point, then a village of perhaps 200 inhabitants, at the present sites of Riverview Shopping Center and the Old Farm apartments. From that vantage point, some soldiers

THE HOME OF WEST POINT MILLER JOHN CABE McCOWN. It was used for target practice by Yankee cavalrymen, camped up the hill and testing their new Spencer repeating rifles. (Courtesy of West Point on the Eno Park.)

CONFEDERATE CAVALRY COMMANDER JOE WHEELER. His troops were remembered "as mean as Yankees" when they retreated through Orange County.

used the home of miller John Cabe McCown for target practice with their new repeating rifles. In any event, West Point became the northern end of Sherman's truce line, which extended through Durham's Station and Chapel Hill, where veterans passing through on their way home from Virginia had brought the news of Appomattox.

The ex-slave Lindsey Faucette described those days:

> Our own soldiers did more harm on our plantation dan de Yankees. Dey camped in de woods and never did have 'nough to eat and took what dey wanted. And lice! I ain't never seed de like. It took 15 years for us to get shed of de lice dat de soldiers left behind. You couldn't get dem out of your clothes 'less you burned dem up.

But Union troops arrived hungry, too. "De first thing dey ask for when dey come was sumpin' to put in dey stomach," Tempie Herndon told Writers' Project interviewer Travis Jordan. "And chicken! I ain't never seed even a preacher eat chicken like dem Yankees."

Some soldiers' appetites, however, were not so basic, as Sarah Debro found when both sides called on the Cain place:

I 'members when Wheelers Cavalry come through. Dey was 'Federates but dey was mean as de Yankees. Dey stole everything dey could find and killed a pile of niggers. Dey come round checkin'. Dey ask de niggers if dey wanted to be free. If dey say no, dey let dem alone. Dey took three of my uncles out in the de woods and shot dey faces off.

I 'members de first time de Yankees come. I was settin' on de steps when a big Yankee come up. He had on a cap and his eyes was mean. "Where did dey hide de gold and silver, nigger?" he yells at me. I was scared and my hands was ashy, but I told him I didn't know nothin' about nothin'; dat if anybody hid things dey hid it while I was sleep.

"Go ask dat ole white headed devil," he said to me. I got mad 'cause he was talkin' about Mis' Polly, so I didn't say nothin'. I jest set. Den he pushed me off de step and say if I didn't dance he gwine shoot my toes off. Scared as I was, I sure done some shufflin'. Den he give me five dollars and told me to go buy jim cracks, but dat piece of paper weren't no good. Twasn't nothin' but a shin-plaster like all dat war money, you couldn't spend it.

Depending on which account one reads, either side gets credit for finding John R. Green's factory.

With thousands of soldiers idled during the surrender talks, and pillaging general in the countryside, good-timing "boys in blue and gray" helped themselves to numerous stores of cured tobacco. However, writing just 19 years after the facts, Hiram Paul established the tradition that it was Green's leaf in particular—stored at Durham's Station just yards from Kilpatrick's headquarters in the home of Dr. Richard Blacknall—that set off the great events to follow.

Green manufactured his product to suit the taste of the college boys. Apparently, it suited the taste of soldiers as well. While their commander Kilpatrick and his aide, a major named Estes, kept company at the Blacknall home with a pair of women "vulgar, rude and indecent"—according to Blacknall's later deposition—Green's factory was, in Paul's words, "completely sacked" for the filling of those pipes of peace.

"Nowhere on the globe is tobacco of such fine quality raised—so peculiarly adapted to smoking purposes—as is grown in the vicinity of Durham," Paul wrote. "It is almost entirely free from nitrates and nicotine."

University boys gone soldiering had already carried Green's Durham smoking tobacco into the field, presumably sharing it with their buddies. Now, boys of the North discovered its qualities. Within weeks, as discharged men got home and smoked up what they had taken with them, enquiries began arriving at the post office and the railroad agency: Where could they get some more?

Meantime, on April 26—the 12th anniversary of the creation of Durham's Station post office—Sherman and Johnston concluded their business at the Bennett farm. Johnston surrendered his 32,000 men, plus 52,000 more Confederates in the Carolinas, Georgia, and Florida. It was the largest

Confederate surrender of the war and was followed shortly by smaller capitulations at Mobile and New Orleans that, for all practical purposes, brought the conflict to an end.

Among the Rebels drifting homeward those springtime weeks, two would play definitive roles in Durham's near future: Julian Shakespeare Carr and Washington Duke. Both men were Methodists: beyond that fact, they were a study in contrasts.

Carr was born in 1845, son of John W. Carr, prosperous merchant of Chapel Hill with interests at Durham's Station. The young Carr was educated, spending two years at the university before enlisting in the Orange Cavalry and becoming part of Lee's command. His regimental historian, Joshua B. Hill, recalled Carr as "a gallant young private," and the flamboyance that would characterize Carr in later life likely attracted him to the horseback service Hill described: "There was something attractive to the younger Southerners in the life of a bold dragoon; especially among those whose life in the open air and participation in field sports had rendered them the finest recruits in the world for this form of military duty."

Paul Means, a courier in the North Carolina Cavalry Brigade, recalled a sortie to secure a railroad bridge on the Meherrin River in southeast Virginia: "Our

PATRIARCH WASHINGTON DUKE. He began a family tobacco business on his farm near Durham's Station after he returned from the War between the States. The business prospered. (Courtesy of the Duke Homestead State Historic Site.)

comrade, Julian S. Carr, was in this charge, to my personal knowledge. I know that Julian S. Carr was in that charge and went as far in it as any man, because I saw and spoke to him then and there and congratulated him on his safety."

The fact that, by the time those words were set down, Carr was rich and famous, carrying the honorary title of "General," may have something to do with the clarity of Hill and Webb's memories.

While Carr journeyed home from Appomattox, Duke was awaiting parole from a prisoner-of-war camp. Born in 1820, the eighth of the ten children of Taylor and Dicey Duke of the Little River country, Washington had received a piece of land as a wedding present in 1842 and gradually enlarged his holding to about 300 acres by 1861. His first wife, Mary Caroline Clinton, died in 1847, leaving Wash with the farm and two small children: Sidney Taylor, 3, and Brodie Leonidas, 1.

Five years later, having put the boys out to live with relatives, Duke met pretty Artelia Roney of Haw River. They married in December 1852, moved into the farmhouse Duke had just built, and began life as a family. Over the next four years, three more children arrived: Mary Elizabeth, Benjamin Newton, and finally, James Buchanan, or "Buck."

Typhoid fever struck the Dukes in 1858. Sidney fell ill, and Artelia took him to her family at Haw River for care. Sidney, however, soon died, and Artelia fatally contracted the fever as well. Duke enlisted female in-laws and a slave woman, Caroline, to help look after the remaining children. As the war approached, Duke, later accounts maintain, opposed secession. Inclination, age, or both kept him out of service until 1863, when he was drafted into the Confederate Navy. Serving on the James River, he was captured during the fall of Richmond.

Decades later, when he was old and rich, Duke recounted his story for a Raleigh newspaper reporter:

> When the war was over, I found myself at Newbern, after being released from Libby prison with only a five dollar Confederate note, sold that to a Federal soldier for fifty cents, and walked home . . . I said to my boys, when I got back home, "The war is over. For people who will do their duty and stick to their business, there never was a better opportunity in the world for men to make their fortunes."

He had a point.

5. Durham's Bull

To complete her memoir *Proud Shoes: The Story of an American Family*, Pauli Murray told a poignant story about paying respect at her grandfather's grave. On Memorial Day, or Decoration Day as it was also called, she would walk up the hill behind her grandparents' home carrying a flag: one lone, little black girl, carrying her lone, little United States flag across Maplewood Cemetery, through a field of Confederate banners.

That was in the 1920s.

Murray's grandfather Robert Fitzgerald was a veteran of Union service. Wounded in the eye while driving an army supply wagon, he was discharged and promptly enlisted in the U.S. Navy. After the war, he came south from Pennsylvania to teach freedmen at University Station, a junction between Durham and Hillsborough where a branch line of the North Carolina Railroad cut off toward Chapel Hill.

Robert was soon followed by his brother Richard, also a Federal veteran. Besides Robert's teaching, the brothers farmed and ran a tannery, and Richard resumed his pre-war occupation as a maker of bricks. In time, Robert joined the brick business, and the brothers received their big break with a contract to supply brick for the new state prison in Raleigh. Soon afterwards, in 1879, they joined the current of enterprise and manpower toward a village to the east that was enjoying a boom nothing short of spectacular.

Much had happened at Durham's Station since Sherman came to call, for black as well as white.

By April 1865, the railroad depot had become the focal point for a village of perhaps 150 souls. Besides John R. Green's tobacco factory, there was Pratt's Gin House, Robert F. Morris's hotel, four stores, three saloons, three schools, two shoemakers—James Whitt, white, and Squire Bull, African American—Baptist and Methodist churches, a machine factory, a sawmill, a stable, a carpenter shop, and at least one blacksmith shop. Aside from blacksmith Lewis Pratt, an African American whose cabin stood approximately at the present intersection of Main and Roxboro Streets, blacks lived toward the edges, but definitely within the community.

Five years later, the population was 256; in a decade, 2,041; and by 1890, more than 5,000. Several factors led to Durham's phenomenal growth. For one thing,

DURHAM BULLS. *Inspired by a jar of mustard, a bull became the emblem for John Green's Durham Smoking Tobacco, and then the symbol for the Bull City. (Courtesy of the Duke Homestead State Historic Site.)*

all across the post-war South, people of all races were drifting out of the impoverished countryside and into the developing industrial towns. Slavery had been replaced by tenant farming and sharecropping, systems that almost inevitably led the landless into ever-deepening debt and, for all practical purposes, conditions of servitude. Land was worn out: cotton and tobacco are both heavy-feeding crops. The cost of fertilizer rose, while the price of farm produce dropped. There was no such thing as crop insurance for a bad year. Even if a man owned his own land, his prospects were, more often than not, bleak. "Public work," in a cotton mill or tobacco plant or one of the subsidiary industries that served them, might be no fit way for a man of the soil to live, but the pay was regular and town offered amenities—schools, for example—that the country could not match.

For another, there was the tobacco business. Tobacco did well by several communities in Reconstruction and the period that followed—Winston, 80 miles west, and Danville, 50 miles north, thrived because of it, but none so well as Durham. Less than 20 years after the exploring soldiers left John Green thinking he was ruined, his company was the biggest producer of smoking tobacco in the United States, with a reputation spreading around the world.

Thanks to a jar of mustard.

In those heady later months of 1865, Green was not the only beneficiary of the sudden demand for "Durham" tobacco. With orders flowing in, everybody wanted into the act and Green found himself in competition with other

66

"manufactories" (shacks and sheds where ambition took the form of flailing dry leaves to pieces) capitalizing on the Durham name and the "Spanish" connection. Green needed a gimmick to set his brand apart.

The story—perhaps apocryphal, but given credence by the Trinity College historian W.K. Boyd for his 1925 *Story of Durham*—is that an acquaintance, inspired by the presence of a new bull in town, suggested that Green adopt that animal's likeness as an emblem. Not long afterward, Green was lunching with a fellow tobacco man, John Y. Whitted, in Hillsborough. As a condiment for their fried oysters, there was a jar of Coleman's Mustard, made in Durham, England, on the table. Whitted noticed that the jar's label carried a picture of a bull, of a breed called "Durham."

According to Boyd, whose book was commissioned by the Chamber of Commerce, Whitted made a suggestion:

> Why not name your product Bull Durham Smoking Tobacco and adopt a whole bull as a trade mark? The mustard must have an immense sale or it would not be found in every store, hotel and restaurant in the country. If you take my advice I predict as wide a market for your product as this mustard has attained, and if it should so prove your fortune will be made and Durham will become a great commercial centre.

Green took the hint. When Whitted was in Durham a few days later, he spotted a sign of the Bull painted on a sheet of iron and set up in front of Green's factory.

Thinking big now, Green took in a partner, William T. Blackwell, a former Roxboro merchant who was prosperous enough to be able to pay a substitute to do his army hitch for him while he went into the tobacco business down east. In 1867, he gave up the tobacco shop he had opened in Kinston and joined Green and, when Green died of consumption two years later, he bought his partner's share of the company.

Blackwell, in turn, took on partners. First James R. Day and then, in 1870, young Julian Carr. Home from the war, Carr had observed his idyllic Chapel Hill disrupted with Reconstruction. The village had been scandalized by the marriage of University of North Carolina president David Swain's daughter Ellie to occupation commander Smith D. Atkins. Plus, the university was broke—$100,000 in debt and no money to pay the faculty—and its enrollment down to 50 for the 1867 fall term. Also, a former professor turned Republican hireling was appointed president in 1869. Racial tension ran high, even in Chapel Hill, and the un-Reconstructed Carr joined in a brawl between freedmen and town boys that left broken limbs and heads, himself whipping an African-American woman who "maligned a Southern lady." Like many others, Carr left. He went west toward the realm of opportunity—and where his uncle had a business in Little Rock.

In all likelihood, fathers being fathers, the elder Carr worried about his boy and what pitfalls and temptations might await him, young, single, and with that dragoon's temperament so near the wild frontier. Perhaps he saw something for himself as well, his own business depressed with the times, when Blackwell and Day went looking for investors. In any case, he bought a third interest in their company for Julian's 25th birthday and the boy was back under his father's watchful eye.

Over the next years, Daddy Carr would get an eyeful.

By the time Julian Carr joined the W.T. Blackwell Company, Durham's Station had officially become a town. Twice over.

In 1866, the village's growth impelled officials of Orange County to seek a charter of its incorporation from the state legislature, which was duly received in December. The following March, the incorporation was rendered null and void when the Reconstruction Congress declared that no legitimate government had existed since 1861 in states formerly in rebellion. With a new, approved state constitution in place, Durham was re-incorporated in April 1869, and this time it stuck. The town's dimensions were specified as reaching half a mile in all directions from the railroad warehouse, at Warehouse (now Corcoran) Street and the track.

For a special "Tobacco Edition" of the Raleigh *News and Observer* in 1896, an essay that appeared over Carr's signature concluded by recalling those beginnings:

> There are men, young yet, who remember the Saturday afternoon when Robert F. Morris, M.A. Angier, Col. D.C. Parrish, Morgan Closs, Washington Duke, Solomon Shepperd, Atlas Riggsbee, J.W. Cheek, Frederick Geer and Col. W.T. Blackwell, with Brown Jordan, a ploughman, and with two big mules laid out Main Street, beginning at Esquire Angier's store [at Main and Mangum] running east through an old field. When their work was done, and two long furrows on either side about a mile long showed where the street was to be, the less credulous of us gathered just as the sun was setting to criticize such foolishness and to guy the 'Fathers' with a refrain as to the price of corner lots and exasperating questions as to how they proposed to people their newly made town. But they builded wiser than they knew, and every one of them lived to see their new-laid street built upon and occupied from end to end.

Cheek became Durham's first mayor, originally titled "Magistrate of Police." Angier, Morris, Riggsbee, W.K. Styron, W.I. Clarke, and William Mangum were the first aldermen, who named J.T. Farthing and Andrew Turner town clerk and constable, respectively. When officials had occasion to meet, it was done in one or another's office or, in good weather, underneath a shady tree between Church and Mangum Streets.

To keep the town running in good order, the aldermen forbade the playing of baseball and marbles on Sunday, as well as Sabbath sales of liquor except for medicinal purposes and any other merchandise besides shrouds for the dead.

JULIAN CARR'S SIGN PAINTERS. The flamboyant Carr dispatched teams of sign painters to make Durham and its Bull known across the United States in the 1870s and 1880s.

Gatherings intended to capture attention or annoy fellow citizens had to conclude at 11 p.m. The issuing of liquor licenses established a tradition of friction between town and county—at first Orange, later Durham—as applicants denied by the aldermen went over their heads to get approval from the commissioners.

Besides plowing the borders of Main Street, the young government went about dignifying the place. Streets formerly known as "Hen Peck Row," "Dog Trot," and "Shake Rag" were re-christened, respectively, "Dillard," "Pettigrew," and "McMannen," the last in honor of the Fiddling Preacher, whose fortunes had recovered to the point that he owned a fine new home in town.

In time, the section of the old Roxboro-to-Fayetteville road, between the northern town limits and the railroad, became Cleveland Street. The road cutting diagonally southwest from the Roxboro road toward Chapel Hill became Green Street, changing to Chapel Hill Street across the track. Mangum Street was designated running south from Green to the track, where it met McMannen Street, thus establishing the tradition of confusion in the names of Durham's thoroughfares.

One other issue arose for the authorities' deliberation.

With growth, and with vagrants attracted to Durham's urban amenities, like the saloons, life was taking its course and the church cemeteries were getting filled to capacity. By 1872, a town cemetery was a pressing need. There was opposition, however, most notably on the part of one Louis Austin, a drifter who had discovered baseball as a Confederate prison guard and felt the public's money would be better spent for a ballpark.

In the election year of 1872, it so happened that the Democrats—read "conservatives" or anti-Reconstructionists—swept Orange County. Caught up in the excitement, some of the town's young bucks, as young bucks will do, began celebrating. With Austin taking enthusiastic part, they found an old cannon and began firing it off as fast as they could load. Unfortunately, their rate of fire was more than the barrel could stand. It overheated, then exploded. Austin was killed and so its most vocal opponent became Maplewood Cemetery's first resident.

A ballpark, however, was eventually laid out across the street. It is nice to think that Austin's spirit enjoyed the games.

All, of course, was not so well in those postbellum years. Occupation troops, Northern missionaries, assorted opportunists, and Republicans appeared, eliciting scorn, fear, and resentment, along with the footloose freedmen sometimes feeling their way, sometimes pushing the envelope to find or determine just what it all really meant for them.

After Southern legislatures tried to restrict the liberties ensured to freedmen by the Fourteenth Amendment, in particular the right to vote, Congressional Reconstruction did some restricting of its own. Local authority in central North Carolina had never recovered from the near-anarchy of early 1865 and after Republican Reconstructionists took over the state government in 1868, the region around Durham's Station saw vigilantism ascendant.

Popular history, more given to the one-liner than to the details in which the devil lives, lumps all postwar efforts at amateur justice under the hood of the Ku Klux Klan. Southern tradition, as affected as any by Hollywood mythology as well as its granddaddy stories, maintains that night-riding and anonymity were called out by general lawlessness. The situation of the late 1860s thus resembles that of

LOUIS AUSTIN'S GRAVE MARKER. The Historic Preservation Society of Durham placed it to remember Austin, who thought the town needed a ballpark more than a cemetery. In 1872, Austin became the public graveyard's first resident.

a century earlier, when Revolutionary civil war opened the way for settling of scores and big-stick law 'n' order.

Caswell County was the scene of a conflict that became known as "Governor Holden's War," in which the state's Republican chief executive called in the militia while a Union League activist, Chicken George, was shot dead on the courthouse steps. Orange County, too, was a busy place after dark. Holden was so disturbed that he asked, and received, the help of Kluxer Pride Jones to calm the rage that had killed five African Americans and sent more emigrating for their lives.

W.T. Redmond, the boy given up by Dr. Durham, came home from Gettysburg and became a Klansman. In 1929, when the Klan was in its second incarnation and at the zenith of its influence (having marched down Pennsylvania Avenue in full regalia and taken over the legislature of Indiana), Redmond and another old-timer, James Lyon, reminisced about their Ku Klux careers for the *Durham Morning Herald*.

Redmond—who by then went by the honorific "Major," though he left the service as but a corporal—told about riding all night to answer a call for help from the Chatham County Klan on a "gangly colt" that was the only mount the thieving Yankees had left behind. He also told of a night visit to a federal prison in Raleigh, where he tossed bottles of beer over the wall to his buddies jailed inside. And then there were the lynchings of Jeff and Dan Morgan, suspected of burning a barn. The men were hung where the barn's owner would see that he was properly avenged when he came out the next morning. Also, Wright Lipscomb, tried and convicted of attacking a white woman, was hung from a dogwood on Johnson Mill Road just down the Little River from South Lowell.

Even without the white vigilantes, times were hard for black folk newly freed. Lindsey Faucette's father was able to buy a farm of his own, but only after several years when, at times, "You couldn't find a crust of bread or piece of meat in my mammy's pantry." Exter and Tempie Herndon bought a farm of their own, too: "We hitched up de wagon and throwed in de passel of chillen and moved to our new farm, and the chillun was put to work in de field. Dey growed up in the field 'cause dey was put to work time dey could walk good."

Sarah Debro was reclaimed by her mother and taken from the Cains' Big House to a "stick and mud house" the Yankees provided:

> It was smoky and dark 'cause dey wasn't no windows. We didn't have no sheets and no towels, so when I cried and said I didn't want to live in no Yankee house, Mammy beat me and made me go to bed. I was never hungry till we was free and de Yankees fed us. I was hungry most of de time and had to keep fightin' off dem Yankee mens.

In her 2001 history of Durham's black "Hayti" district, *End of an Era*, Dorothy Phelps Jones quotes a tradition that African Americans, drifting into the village after Emancipation, were relegated by whites to the other, southern, side of the tracks with the sentiment, "Put them over there, they'll be dead in 50 years."

On the "white side" of the tracks, the tradition goes that since Durham was practically starting from scratch in 1865, the town had no antebellum baggage as did such older communities as Hillsborough, Raleigh, and Chapel Hill, and so in Durham, opportunity was open to all who were willing to work.

Traditions come down with the benefit of hindsight and the reshaping to suit what each succeeding generation thinks it needs in the way of historical sanction. The pre–Civil War distribution of free blacks in Orange County and proto-Durham, however, lends some support to the open-opportunity point of view. Analyzing the war's effects on kinship and neighborhood, the historian Robert Kenzer found no evidence that whites were unwilling to sell real estate, wherever they had it to sell, to anyone who could pay for it.

Robert Fitzgerald, the African-American teacher turned brickmaker, recorded that when his father came south and wanted to buy property, he was courted by numerous white landowners offering good deals. Eventually, the elder Fitzgerald bought a 158-acre farm. Kenzer did find, however, that most of the African Americans who did well after the war were of mixed ancestry: most antebellum free blacks had white blood and mulattoes made up a disproportionate share of the non-white force of skilled labor.

In any case, some freedmen did give up on life in the country and move into the developing tobacco town. By 1870, there were almost 700 African Americans in the Durham Township of Orange County, about half of the white population at the time: by 1880, the ratio was two to three. Many of the new African-American residents came from the Bennehan-Cameron lands just to the north, including most of the buyers in the area that would become Hayti—below the tracks, southwest of the intersection of the Fayetteville Road and Railroad (later Pettigrew) Street, which ran downslope from and parallel to the track. White neighbors south of the tracks included merchants M.A. Angier and J.W. Cheek, Dr. Richard Blacknall, and the Reverend McMannen.

One likely reason for African-American settlement in that area was the presence of two churches founded by blacks. In 1866, Margaret Faucette, a self-educated former slave, widow, and mother of 13, came to Durham from Hillsborough and began hosting prayer meetings at her home in a Pettigrew Street rooming house. In good weather, worship moved to a brush arbor outdoors. Two years later, under leadership of Reverend Samuel Hunt, services moved into a small building down the street and Faucette put the first dollar into a church building fund.

Also in 1868, Edian Markum (also spelled "Markham") came to Durham's Station. A native of northeastern North Carolina—accounts differ on whether Elizabeth City or Edenton was his hometown, and whether Markum was born slave or free—he moved or was taken to Ohio. He learned to read, tradition says, from a spelling book and a dictionary and then got the call to preach.

Arriving in Durham, he bought a piece of land, built a cabin for himself and a brush arbor for his ministry, "fixed with poles buried in the grassy earth." In 1870, called to further missions, he deeded the property to the congregation he had gathered. Markum's brush arbor grew into St. Joseph's African Methodist Episcopal Church. Faucette's prayer meetings grew into White Rock Baptist Church. These two, the original black churches in Durham, became and continue to be power centers of the black community, spiritual home to the movers and shapers, visionaries, and money men in what became a mecca for African-American enterprise, with its upper crust residing along the Fayetteville Street ridge, looking down upon and in clear view of the neighborhoods and businesses below.

This mecca was not made without encouragement and help from across the way. The patronage bestowed by Durham's white tycoons upon their African-American fellow entrepreneurs is sometimes held up as a mark of liberality in the characters of Washington Duke, Julian Carr, and their associates. Sometimes, as noblesse oblige—clearly and unspokenly little different from the plantation paternalism that informed the New Southerners' approach to running factories and railroads—and sometimes as social conscience, if not enlightened self-interest. That's on the north side of the railroad. On the south side, tradition with the status of common knowledge affirms that the interest of rich white men in ambitious black men was due to kinship literally as well as economically. Fathers

EVANGELIST EDIAN MARKUM. He arrived at Durham's Station in 1868, buying a lot and founding a brush-arbor church there, which grew into the influential Saint Joseph's A.M.E. congregation. (Courtesy of Hayti Heritage Center.)

73

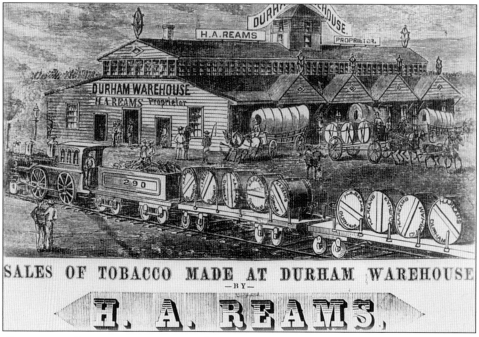

SALES OF TOBACCO MADE AT DURHAM WAREHOUSE
—by—
H. A. REAMS.

Engraved Advertisement for One of Durham's Early Auction Houses. Opened in 1871, the Durham tobacco market assured producers of a steady supply of leaf and farmers of competitive prices without traveling to Virginia. (Courtesy of Duke Homestead State Historic Site.)

would do as right as their senses of propriety, conscience, and pragmatism would allow by the secret sons of their unofficial second families.

African Americans, of course, understood the game that everyone was playing and gave credit where it was due, expedient, and good business. When a splendid new St. Joseph's rose in Fitzgerald brick atop the Fayetteville Street ridge in 1892, Washington Duke's likeness beamed down upon the sanctuary from a stained-glass window. When White Rock Baptist opened its equally fine new building in 1896, the preacher was Trinity College professor W.H. Pegram and Ol' Wash was a special guest. White Rock's minister, Allen Eaton, told it like it was to Duke: "You have given us more cash money than any man."

By that time, Duke, Carr, and their associates had plenty of money to go around. Already in the 1870s, Durham was becoming a place of social and economic diversity.

Notwithstanding the annoyance of a series of litigations over trademark infringement regarding the use of a bull symbol and the word "Durham"—by manufacturers in and out of town—the Bully triumvirate of Blackwell, Carr, and Day expanded in 1871 into the marketing business.

Nearby growers benefited from tobacco manufacturing at Durham's Station. They could sell their crop at the factory door, rather than hauling it the laborious and time-consuming miles to market in Virginia. This, however, was an erratic system both in terms of supply and demand. Ensuring a steady and adequate supply of leaf still required buying trips north. For farmers, prices at the door were less than what they could get in organized markets elsewhere. Blackwell suggested, and his partners agreed, that they build a warehouse and introduce auction buying at Durham, a win-win proposition for the parties on either side of the transaction.

Opening day, May 17, was a sign of things to come. For village residents, it was like a carnival, with farm wagons rattling into town before the sun was up, setting off an alarm from dogs, hogs, and chickens. The spectacle was worth getting up for, as auctioneer Ed Parrish strode the warehouse floor dressed in white pants, shirt, and Panama hat, mustachioed and goateed, and on cue broke into the selling chant that would become famous.

That first day moved 50,000 pounds of tobacco; the first season, 700,000; the next year, 2 million; and the Blackwell Company had to build a bigger warehouse. In 1873, a second warehouse opened and in 1874, a third, as Parrish struck out on his own. By 1880, there were two more. With expansion and growth came enterprises of service and support: brokers, sign-painters, itinerant entertainers, saloons, retailers, an insurance agency, and notably, the town's first bank (opened in 1878 by Eugene Morehead, son of a former governor). Making cotton bags for tobacco was a cottage industry that would lead Durham into full-fledged textile manufacturing in the 1880s.

The village's evangelically Protestant character was broken, too. Presbyterians organized a congregation in 1871 and on Sunday, May 26, 1878, the Reverend Joseph Cheshire, deacon of the Episcopal Chapel of the Cross in Chapel Hill, walked the 10 miles to Durham to lead morning prayer for 10 worshippers in an upper room above a store. Cheshire's hike became a monthly routine and foundation of St. Philip's Episcopal Church followed. In March 1874, the brothers Abe and Jacob Goldstein opened their "Jew Store," where they advertised a "large and attractive stock of general merchandise." The best calico went for 10¢ a yard, calfskin boots $3 to $5, and ladies underskirts 60¢ to 75¢. Durham even had a Chinese laundryman.

In the 1870s, Durham gained fraternal orders: Knights of Pythias, Good Templars, Masons, and Odd Fellows. John Green's brother Caleb started the town's first newspaper, the *Tobacco Plant*, in 1872, and seven years later, new owner John Cameron moved the 59-year-old *Hillsborough Recorder* to Durham. Political fevers were still running high as Democrats (a.k.a. Conservatives) contended to wring out all vestige of Republican ("Radical") power. The *Tobacco Plant* editorialized in 1875:

> Mr. W. Duke has been induced to again take the field as the Republican candidate in Orange for a seat in the Convention. One by one they are laid on the shelf and in a few years Republican candidates in Orange will be as scarce as hen's teeth. This is a Democratic people and it will be

late when they can be induced to vote for Radical sailing under Republican colors.

Conventional hindsight assumes that racial segregation, the system that was undone by the 1960s, dropped fully armed from the brow of Jim Crow as soon as the Yankees left the South. This is not true. While white supremacy was the prevailing attitude among white people—North and South, however kindly or angrily disposed they were toward African-American people—civil rights and black enfranchisement remained hot and open issues for 30 years after Reconstruction. Still, mythologies that would affirm current prejudice and shape future belief were being deliberately set in place.

For example, the April 28, 1875 *Tobacco Plant*'s "interview" with "Uncle Billy, a good old colored friend," targeted the question of civil rights:

> Don't want nuffin mo.' Got too much already . . . We're ekal befo' de law, an' dar you hit our weak point. Befo' the waw, if [one of us] stole chicken an' pig . . . guv him thirty-nine lashes, an' let him go. But jist let a cullud pusson try it now? They hauls him 'fore court, and sends him to the penitentiary, jest like he was one of your poor white trash.
>
> Mars Boss, we can't run agin natur'. It's nat'ral for niggas to steal pig and chicken fryin' size.

The writer suggested to Uncle Billy the following:

> the colored people were indebted to their republican friends for this change of their status.
>
> "Well, den, Mars' Boss, all I got to say is, de law is got to be changed. Must hab a law for de white man and a law for de black man."
>
> Strange as it may seem, some of our best citizens echo Uncle Billy's sentiments.

For all its coming urbanity, Durham in the 1870s remained a small town where farms coexisted alongside the chugging, whistling, and banter of commerce. S.H. Webb won a year's subscription to the *Tobacco Plant* for raising the heaviest watermelon of the 1875 season at 33 pounds. Rustic manners prevailed as well. The same September 8 edition of the newspaper that announced Webb's award carried a stern rebuke:

> We hear many of our young ladies complaining of the way some of the young men scatter tobacco juice over the church floors. This is a very ugly practice and we are surprised that *any* one would be guilty of such. It would be advisable for those who can't refrain from using the weed while in church to occupy seats where the ladies have no occasion to go, as the ambier is very destructive of their dresses.

6. Everything's Up to Date

The original Duke of Durham was Brodie, eldest of Wash's three boys. At 96 pounds, Brodie was considered too scrawny for frontline duty when he enlisted in the Confederate cause, so he spent his hitch doing guard duty at the prisoner-of-war camp in Salisbury. By the spring of 1865, he would have seen and experienced a lot for a boy of 19—the barbaric conditions of a military prison and the loss of his mother and stepmother both. Perhaps these events endowed Brodie with a lasting rebel streak, a mind of his own, or maybe something more.

After the war, he joined in the family's tobacco business, his father having quickly realized there was better money in processing the leaf than actually growing it. When he tried to convince Wash to move their operation into the thriving village 3 miles away, however, the elder Duke declined and, in 1869, Brodie left home.

The two-and-a-half story brick warehouse that Brodie had built in 1878 is the oldest tobacco warehouse in Durham, still standing at Corporation and Liggett Streets and lately remodeled for office space. The Trinity Park, Duke Park, and North Durham neighborhoods were Brodie's developments on land he bought against his father's advice. He built the Pearl Cotton Mill and its associated village along the Belt Line railroad he had built to get around an extended right-of-way dispute downtown. When the *Durham Recorder* newspaper brought out a "salute to industry" edition in April 1890, Brodie's spread was as long as that of any of the town's other men of business, including his father.

But that's not what Brodie is remembered for. Once upon a time, the family was concerned because Brodie had taken up with a woman of dubious reputation. Little half-brother James Buchanan was delegated to set him straight. "Brodie," the younger Duke began, "don't you know that woman's been to bed with every man in Durham?"

"Hell, Buck," Brodie replied. "Durham ain't that big."

In 1879, having made a go of his own business, Brodie rejoined the firm of W. Duke Sons & Company, which had just taken in an outside partner, finance man George W. Watts from Baltimore. In 1884, the terms of partnership were redefined. All the principals agreed to put $2,000 a year into the business except Brodie, who was excused in exchange for the pledge to "conduct himself in such a manner as to reflect credit upon the firm and not to drink liquors to intoxication."

Brothers Buck and Ben enjoyed their good times, too, the stories tell, but they had the good grace and common decorum to have them out of town, often at a fishing camp near the coast. Brodie's antics had already included a lawsuit for breach of promise to marry—settled for $500—and riding his horse into the family factory. Brodie was independent, colorful, one day flush and the next day broke, an early enlistee in the distinguished roll of Durham's town characters.

It is not unlikely that Brodie's feelings were hurt and he resented Watts for usurping his position in the family and, perhaps, in his father's affections. Maybe there was some offense in the business. At any rate, Brodie harbored a grudge along with his sense of fun. In 1895, Watts built and donated to the city its first hospital, which stood at the edge of Brodie's property west of town. Six years later, Brodie began developing the area for residences. As developer, it was his privilege to name the streets he had laid out, which he did so that the plat, filed at the courthouse, read east to west: "Washington, Duke, Hated, Watts."

That boy, that boy, that boy. Evidently, the family had another little talk with Brodie. The name "Hated" was promptly changed to "Gregson" in honor of the Dukes' preacher.

Watts's hospital had been sorely needed, along with a number of other urban amenities Durham was just acquiring toward the end of the nineteenth century.

BRODIE LEONIDAS. Eldest of Washington Duke's sons, he was the first of the family to leave the farm and set up a tobacco business at Durham's Station, 3 miles from home.

Bully Durham, through the 1870s and 1880s when its first fortunes were being built, was a filthy place. In rainy weather, mud rose over pedestrians' ankles, seasoned with the leavings of horses and mules. Flies frolicked and bred in and about the deposits of outdoor privies and the pigpens decorating residential yards. The town's first attempt at a sanitation commission failed for lack of interest. Neighboring towns referred to typhoid as "Durham Fever." However one felt about the fragrance of tobacco—"Smells like money" was the local proverb—there was no arguing that the town stank to high heaven.

Meantime, Durham carried on the traditions and reputations of Prattsburg and Pinhook. A court declared the fists of saloon-keeper Leander Rochelle to be deadly weapons. It was said that an early mayor, when the office doubled as police magistrate, fined himself for presiding drunk in his own courtroom. Another tale has Mayor W.J.H. Durham, having primed himself before church one Sunday morning, loudly informing the preacher when he had sermonized enough. The preacher quickly pronounced the benediction.

Dispensing of spirits was not only a point of city and county contention, it was a vital cog in the economy. Institutions such as Carrington's, Jim's Place, and Happy Patty's comfortably outnumbered Durham's churches. In 1869, after Methodist minister R.S. Webb led an unsuccessful campaign to close the town's saloons, the saloon owners offered Webb's landlord $20 a month more for the preacher's lodgings than Webb was paying. Unable to match the extra rent, for what were the only rooms to let in town, Webb was forced to move to Chapel Hill and commute to tend his flock.

Downhill to the east, in the present Edgemont, was Durham's brothel district. Its geography closely fit the description of Eugene Gant's introduction to the pleasures of the flesh during an adventure from "Pulpit Hill" to "Exeter," in Thomas Wolfe's autobiographical novel *Look Homeward, Angel.* The whorehouses lay just beyond Dillard and Cleveland Streets, which were lined with the Victorian mansions of Durham's new rich.

(Those icons of respectability liked to have their little games, too. Turn-of-the-century Durham photographer Hugh Mangum was occasionally engaged for parties at the rich folks' homes where they would have their pictures made in positions of undress and compromise. Unfortunately, it is said, the photographer's heirs destroyed the negatives.)

Among those stately homes, stateliest was Somerset Villa on Dillard Street at the east end of Main, with a view back toward downtown as if to keep an eye on business. In 1887 and 1888, Julian Carr lavished $125,000 on construction of his Queen Anne edifice, which replaced his Italianate Waverly Honor, built on the same 5-acre lot less than 15 years earlier. Ever inclined to impress, Carr assured architect John Halcott that money was no object and only the best would do. For his assurance, he received towers, bays, gables, turrets, wood, stone, gingerbread, marble, slate, bronze, and more. According to biographer Mena Webb, the 41-year-old millionaire spent $5,000 on chandeliers, $6,000 on stained-glass windows, and $40,000 on furniture and rugs. He then hired European

SOMERSET VILLA. Julian S. Carr's second mansion was built on Dillard Street in 1887 and 1888, costing $125,000. (Courtesy of Durham County Public Library.)

landscapers, who populated his gardens with such familiars as crepe myrtles and magnolias and such exotics as banana and coffee trees. Palmettos—really north of their comfort zone—lined the front walk, and carnations and roses for the great man's lapels grew year-round in his greenhouse.

Such Nouveau-Southern flamboyance worked even upon the un-Reconstructed gentility of Cornelia Phillips Spencer, who deigned to accept Carr's invitation down to Durham in March 1889. Afterward, she wrote fellow aristocrat Paul Cameron that she "found the house & its fittings well worth a visit," including the silver bathroom fixtures and furnishings "all on the costliest scale." Nonetheless, the grand lady of Chapel Hill could not resist a telling dig: "Some one has wondered why Mr. C. should choose to put such a house & such furniture in such a place as Durham. But here it is unique."

Carr's baronial ostentation may have, even by standards of the Gilded Age, bordered on tacky, but it was symbolically fitting. Flamboyance and showmanship had made him the richest man in North Carolina, as it had made Bull Durham the best known name in smoke. The Blackwell Company built a new factory in 1874 with the permanence of brick and an exterior "pretentiously stylish" (in the words of the building's nomination, a century later, as a National Historic Landmark). Its young principal embarked on a nationwide ad campaign the like of which no Carolina product had enjoyed before. "It ain't no use to tell me that advertising don't pay," Carr wrote Blackwell in 1877. "I have studied advertising hard, and am satisfied about it."

First, Carr went after celebrity endorsements and secured them from, among others, the Reverend W.J. Milburn, chaplain to the United States Senate; Alfred Lord Tennyson, poet laureate of Great Britain; and Alexander H. Stephens, vice president of the Confederacy. Then, he placed advertisements in rural weekly newspapers and major city dailies across the Republic; gave away premiums with purchase, such as razors and Bull Soap; and offered cash for return of empty Bull Durham bags.

Then there were the signs, which appeared on barns and fences and just about anything that would stand still as Carr kept four teams of painters busy from New England to Texas to the Pacific Northwest and even across the water. One legend from that era holds that the baseball term "bullpen" originated with a Bull Durham billboard that stood behind the New York Yankees' dugout. Another, that Mark Twain's most memorable impression of Egypt was the Durham Bull painted across one of the pyramids.

Between Carr's promotions and the triumvirate's management savvy, growth came so fast that the new factory had to be enlarged in 1880, thus becoming the biggest tobacco plant in the world. In 12 years, the company had risen from a dozen hired hands to more than 900. Every day, 25,000 pounds of Bull Durham left the plant—more than a boxcar full; each year, 5 million pounds.

Carr, by the way, had no monopoly on flair. Blackwell had constructed a factory whistle with a calliope-like contraption that put out a sound like a roaring bull.

A SITTING ROOM INSIDE CARR'S SOMERSET VILLA. In the Durham of the 1880s, the lavish residence was unique and its ostentatiousness fit its owner's personality. (Courtesy of Durham County Public Library.)

"The effect on strangers who are not aware of the existence of an artificial bellower is remarkable," reported the *Greensboro Patriot* of March 8, 1876. Morning, noon, and night, the bull let loose and the sound could be heard for miles—when conditions were right, probably as far as Chapel Hill.

Such prosperity, in a smelly little whistle stop that had emerged in no time from less than nowhere, naturally elicited some feelings of envy and more of disdain on the part of piedmont communities enjoying their postwar privations with stoic righteousness.

Kenneth Boyd summed up the sentiments in his 1925 *Story of Durham*:

> Durham was generally regarded as a dirty town, its people as uncultivated, its leading citizens as sordid and devoted to the worship of mammon. Historic, aristocratic Hillsborough regarded it as distinctly second class. Classic Chapel Hill viewed it with disdain. Cultured but politic Raleigh lifted an eyebrow when it was mentioned.

However, there is little arguing with success. In Durham, according to the *Tobacco Plant*, a new home was built every month in 1876; by 1878, it was a new one every week; by 1880, one a day. Its Orange County rival, the *Recorder* of aristocratic Hillsborough, was forced to admit in print that the "insignificant hamlet" had become an "important town" from which lessons were to be drawn:

> Its growth and its prosperity teach us what manufacturing can do for a country by the stimulus it gives industrial life; and also the wisdom of a diversity of pursuit by departing with discreet adventure from the old and worn highways of commerce and agriculture, the ancient trusted road to wealth and independence.

Indeed, citizens of the 129-year-old county seat could do little more than huff and puff over the disrespect paid "Old Orange" when Durham interests began pushing for secession.

As a commercial center, Durham had far outstripped Hillsborough by 1880. While the colonial hub drifted into sweet nostalgia, the roaring old place roared on, but to register a deed, file a lawsuit, or fulfill a jury obligation required a full-day round trip, even by train, from Durham. Time was money.

In 1881, thanks to some ill-advised power plays among the county's political set, it happened that Orange County's entire delegation to the North Carolina General Assembly was from its eastern half. Durham interests were quick to take advantage of this and, with a bit of parliamentary maneuvering and a lot of back-room deal-making, the legislature authorized the creation of Durham County on February 28. The voters made it official on April 10. Wake and Granville Counties opposed this change (Granville at the time was facing its own secession movement from the incipient Vance County).

Meanwhile, that Bull-based prosperity was also inspiring competition.

EAST MAIN STREET IN THE 1870S. The church on the left is Durham's first First Presbyterian, which still occupies the same position at Main and Roxboro. (Courtesy of Durham County Public Library.)

Brodie Duke had come to town in 1869 and set up his tobacco works in an old house on Main Street. Its downstairs room became his factory and its upstairs room his warehouse with space left for a bed. His first brand was called "Semper Idem," which means "Always the same." His second was "Duke of Durham" and, in those struggling years, he lived the straight and narrow life—according to a newspaper tribute years later—subsisting on hoecake, bacon, and "the pure unadulterated ale of father Adam—branch water."

It is not recorded whether Brodie ever told his father "I told you so," but in 1874 the rest of the Dukes—Washington, daughter Mary, and sons Ben and Buck—sold the farm and came to town. They shared production facilities, such as they were, with Brodie, but kept their businesses separate for five more years.

By that time, Brodie had built his brick warehouse, bought a store building, and opened a furniture company that sold the brand-new county the tables, chairs, and whatall for its first courtroom and poorhouse. He was good at business and he was lucky. Once, he went on a leaf-buying trip for the family firm and got drunk along the way. When the tobacco he had bought arrived in Durham, it was missing the cards that show the quality grade of each batch. Brodie just put it all together and called it "Duke's Mixture." It was the company's bestselling brand for years.

Posterity knows Brodie as the black sheep of the Dukes. In truth, he was a worry to his father and trouble again and again for his siblings. Today, while Wash, Ben, and Buck rest in Duke Chapel, Brodie remains in the old family mausoleum at Maplewood Cemetery. Preaching at a Durham revival in 1897, a Methodist evangelist said, "Let us pray very earnestly for Brodie. I used to know him before I became a Christian."

Brodie's luck could fail him. Having an unfortunate appetite for commodity speculation, he was virtually wiped out in the depression of 1893, the year after he came home from an Illinois alcohol clinic "sober as a judge." Brother Ben took over Brodie's interest in one cotton mill, George Watts another and, adding insult to injury, his sister Mary, to whom Brodie was devoted, died.

Seven years later, Brodie was back on his financial feet. The *Recorder* wrote a tribute:

> There is a lesson to be learned from Mr. Duke's life. The symbolism of all earnest living and striving is a wrestling nip and tuck with adverse circumstances, and it is in the struggles of the wrestling that skill and strength are won. The hero of to-day is one who never yields, who conquers circumstance, who snatches success from failure and wrests victory from defeat.

Brodie did live his life earnestly. By 1900, he owned eight stores built of brick, made fashionable in Durham after the town's quick-buck wood structures fed a series of disastrous fires. He owned houses, lots, and the real estate he was soon to develop north and west of town. He also owned half interest in a tobacco warehouse in Durham, 25,000 acres of land in Chatham and Orange Counties, more property in Asheville and Newport News, Virginia, and he had built a railroad in Tennessee.

WOMEN HAND-ROLLING CIGARETTES. In this 1870s tobacco factory, a top roller might turn out 2,000 smokes in an 11-hour day. (Courtesy of Duke Homestead State Historic Site.)

Brodie even donated the land on Main Street for a Methodist church, which had started as a Sunday school in his father's factory. He married Martha McMannen, daughter of the Fiddling Preacher, and built for her a mansion befitting his stature near the family factory at present Morgan and Duke Streets, now the campus of the Durham School of the Arts, whose athletic field lies across the bottom of Brodie's backyard goldfish pond. Martha McMannen Duke died in 1888, leaving Brodie with three children. He remarried in 1890 to Alabama socialite Minnie Woodward, with whom he had one more child before their divorce in 1904. His third marriage was brief, entered into during a two-week party after brother Buck's wedding in New York. Brodie maintained that he remembered nothing of his wedding to Alice Webb, which was held on December 19, 1904 at Madison Square Presbyterian Church. He soon obtained a divorce, after his brothers had committed him to a sanitarium and engaged legal assistance. He married for the last time in 1910: he was 63 and Wylanta Rochelle was 18. The book *Durham Illustrated*, published that year, described Brodie as "a gentleman of standing."

Brodie would go on to become a patron of the National Religious Training School and Chautauqua, now North Carolina Central University. He gave money, land, or both for a Presbyterian Church near his Pearl Mill and a home for elderly ladies in his Trinity Park. Nevertheless, when Washington Duke, late in life, began distributing assets among his heirs, he put Brodie's share into a trust fund. The boy was buying cotton futures.

With all its ups and downs and its widespread interests, Brodie's career is a far better metaphor for that of his adopted city than those of his more respectable kinfolk. Brodie was the one boy who stayed in Durham. Buck moved to New York in 1884, there creating and running the American Tobacco Trust. Ben spent most of his time in New York, though he did maintain a Durham home, Four Acres, that rivaled Carr's in splendor. Brodie fooled around, made money, lost money, and made it again in one enterprise after another. Buck early on fixed his ambition on taming the Bull.

One of Buck Duke's inspired ideas was to concentrate on cigarettes. Up into the 1870s, tobacco was manufactured and sold either as plugs or twists for chewing or loose for tamping into pipes. Cigarettes were invented and caught on in Europe in the 1850s, reached New York during the Civil War, and gradually won favor across the country. Buck saw a niche he could occupy and, therefore, how he could go after the dominating Blackwell Company.

In 1881, following the Bull's lead, he went to New York and hired about 125 East European Jews experienced in the trade to come roll cigarettes in Durham. Hand-rolling was a slow process. In a working day of 11 or so hours, a top roller could turn out about 2,000 cigarettes. It was also labor-intensive. In those days, labor could mean trouble.

Blackwell and company had already experienced a strike in August 1875, but, fresh off the farm, its employees had no understanding of labor economics. The *Greensboro Patriot* reported that the Bull's factory hands "struck work about breakfast time and walked out of the house." The company simply dispatched a labor recruiter, Bill Hammit, who quickly returned from Virginia with "40 picked hands" to take the strikers' places.

Recent immigrants, however, brought seditious notions about labor, management, and revolutions into the workplace, which employed children as young as eight years old who had, the nominally boosterish Hiram Paul wrote in a Knights of Labor publication, whips applied to their backs when they got behind on the job. Whatever the truth of that charge, James B. Duke did pay a call on the Knights' headquarters, where he struck an agreement for kinder and gentler managers if labor organizers would leave his help alone.

In a Raleigh newspaper's 1896 Tobacco Edition, Washington Duke would recall that the Jewish rollers "gave us no end of trouble," especially after Buck decided to mechanize. For years, tinkerers had tried to devise a machine to make cigarettes, but all the prototypes were prone to constant breakdowns. In 1884, Duke learned of a reliable machine invented by Virginian James Bonsack that could match the daily production of 48 hand rollers without complaints, bathroom breaks, or ideas of their own. Buck Duke made another deal by which he could lease Bonsack's machines at an exclusive cut rate. Then, for insurance, he hired away the one mechanic, W.T. O'Brien, who could keep the Bonsacks running.

O'Brien and his tech crew were threatened by the hand rollers, as were the vile machines themselves, and agitators agitated for a boycott on Duke products. Little but annoyance came of it. W. Duke Sons & Company did keep a few hand rollers for a while, just in case, but in 1885, they were directed to cut their production to 1,000 cigarettes a day. The rollers were paid by the cigarette. As further hint, rollers claimed, Duke required them to deposit their compensation for 1,000 cigarettes a week into the company's missionary fund. By 1886, all but two of the immigrants had gone back to New York, just in time for machines to put them out of work there, too. Thereafter, what labor was required was recruited from "natives."

(The tradition that Duke's rollers were the foundation of Durham's Jewish community is false: the community grew rapidly after the Goldstein brothers' arrival in 1874, but it was primarily made up of merchants and their families.)

If Duke's "trouble" with the rollers was not enough to give organized labor a bad name in Durham, a local tobacco worker was implicated in Chicago's violent Haymarket riot of 1886. Police scouring a "radical" office found a note, signed by one J.A. Strickland of Durham and addressed from the Durham Knights of Labor office, proclaiming "Vive le Commune" and predicting the red flag would fly over Bull City. Strickland denied writing the letter, but accused Raleigh organizer John Ray of being an anarchist. Ray denied the charge, Strickland recanted, and it was a farfetched charge in the first place, for Ray had earlier warned North Carolina that false agents were holding public meetings to promote "communistic and revolutionary doctrines." Before long, labor agitation would be taken care of by linking it, in the Southern mind, with other darker powers.

His Bonsacks rolling away, Duke's company was far out-producing the Bull and profitably selling his cigarettes at a fraction of the competition's price. Settling into New York City with the era's other empire builders, Buck Duke, over the next few years, bought and arm-twisted 90 percent of the United States cigarette industry into his American Tobacco Company, then started mopping up the chewing business, too. His trophies included R.J. Reynolds of Winston-Salem and, in 1899, the Bull itself. His monopoly would rule until the Supreme Court broke it up in 1911.

With James B. Duke's departure and northern consolidation, control of the industry that had built the town went out of town. It was an age, as the 1895 *Hand-Book of Durham* expressed it, of "sharp competition." But as the 1880s moved along and blended into the 1890s, Durham's economy was diversifying. In the year of the Bonsacks, Julian S. Carr started the Durham Cotton Manufacturing Company, capitalizing on the tobacco factories' need for bag cloth, and around it grew a new village, East Durham. Ben Duke started his cotton mill in 1892 and around Erwin Mill, named for its manager, formed the village of West Durham. Two hosiery mills opened in 1894, merged in 1898, and formed the

JAMES B. DUKE. Buck Duke is shown here on a fishing trip in eastern North Carolina. (Courtesy of the Duke Homestead State Historic Site.)

DURHAM COUNTY POOR FARM. This institution for the destitute was one of the first creations of the new Durham County after its separation from "old Orange" in 1881. (Courtesy of the Durham County Public Library.)

basis for the Edgemont community down in the old red-light district. Lumber and flour mills came on line, as did more banks and railroads.

Durham was taking on a veneer of up-to-dateness and respectability. Besides the county's poor farm north of town, the 1880s brought a municipal water system that tapped the Eno River, feeding businesses and homes through a 6-mile pipeline. Plus, a Lyceum society stimulated and expanded the local mind. Home mail delivery began in 1890 and founding postman John L. Kirkland served his route until 1936. Baseball, the game of choice of the unfortunate Louis Austin, was being played for funsies by the mid-1870s when the Durham Base Ball Club opposed the Eno Bottom Rangers of Hillsborough. The game became a professional fixture in 1902 with the first edition of the Durham Bulls. Julian Carr built the fabulous Carrolina Hotel beside the railroad tracks in 1891, a 73-room Queen Anne structure with frescoes and period decor in its guests' rooms. A horse-drawn streetcar line began service in 1887, two years after Carr, Watts, and Eugene Morehead formed an electric-power company.

There were even attempts at prohibition, which gained victories when Durham County officially went dry in 1888, followed by the whole state in 1908. Thus forced, the saloon trade went behind closed doors where its establishments became known as "blind tigers." It would be generations before Durham's Methodists and Baptists could again drink in front of each other.

Southgate Jones Sr. was born in 1888 to tobacco man Thomas Decatur Jones and his wife Mattie Southgate. In his memoir *Glancing Back from the House on*

Chapel Hill Street, Jones described his boyhood home: hearth of Oriental tile, chandelier of alabaster, indoor bathroom and well, and a conservatory stocked with wonders such as preserved sea creatures, gold dust from the Klondike, a black opal from California, and cameos from the court of Louis XVI. Outside there were gardens of fountains, exotic shrubs, and fruit trees. All in all, "quiet majesty in sharp contrast to steam trains and rum-smelling tobacco factories across the street."

The Durham of the Gilded Age was a place of sharp contrast, as well as sharp competition. Amusement for young Jones and his playmates included the breeding and training of fighting cocks. With the trappings of civility there endured the spirit of the roaring old place.

In October 1888, the town showed itself off to itself with an Exposition that advertised:

> Liberal premiums for tobacco!
> Dazzling display of fireworks!
> Magnificent street parade!
> Confederate re-union!

Guests included North Carolina senators Vance and Ransom and Governor Gorden of Georgia. On opening day, the *Recorder* reported the following:

> The people have come to witness Durham's gala demonstration and exhibits. They are here, and they are here by the thousands. They have come from the country, and from neighboring towns. Trains have been emptying them here at our depot, throughout the day, and we may say the population of Durham to-day is about 15,000.

On an ordinary day, the population was one-third of that number. Just a few weeks later, business was suspended and thousands more flocked for salvation as Sam Jones, "the great evangelist" from Georgia, preached five evenings in the Parrish Warehouse. Jones's sermons were seasoned with pithy exclamations, such as:

"Whiskey! Whiskey! Oh, boys, don't drink it, don't do that. Let a man who has been to the very gates of hell beg of you, stop."

and

"Here's my theology: If you seek it you'll find it and if you find it you'll know you've got it and if you've got it you can lose it and if you lose it you've had it."

or

"We preachers ought to be about 99 percent man and 1 percent preacher."

Just days after Sam Jones delivered his final benediction, election day arrived. It culminated a hard-fought and critical campaign, since the "boss Rads" of Durham County had, in integrated convention, nominated Dr. Aaron Moore, "colored," for the office of coroner.

"White men of Durham," called the *Durham Recorder*, "those who have any respect for the Anglo-Saxon race, will you fail to do your duty on the 6th of November? Will you allow Negro rule or a white man's government?"

The troops thus roused, the competing *Tobacco Plant* of November 9 could crow, "Durham County Redeemed; Democratic from one end to the other." Jubilation was quickly tempered the night after the election when the home of Democratic Executive Council Chairman C.B. Green was set afire with kerosene, "used to make more certain," said the *Plant*, now owned by Julian Carr, "the devilish work of the villain. The probable cause of the work of these demons appears in an article on the editorial page of this issue."

Actually, the editorials were just on the other side of the same page. The newspaper issued the following opinion:

> The negro, if he would, is not allowed to vote the Democratic ticket, for fear of serious bodily harm, if not actual death at the hands of the colored people. Not content with this, if a white man dare be active and works prominently in the interest of the Democratic party, he is liable to have his helpless wife and children turned homeless into the street at dead of night, by the burning torch. White men, in name of God, how can you do otherwise than stand by your white neighbor!

In the next item, the *Plant* urged "the great importance of following wise counsel and keeping cool for the next few days."

The *Recorder* ascribed the deed to "enraged darkies." In the next few days, rumor settled responsibility upon blacksmith E.G. Jordan, former Radical candidate for constable and alderman and, moreover, a visible Knight of Labor. Jordan was collared by night by a lynch mob, but E.J. Parrish, the flamboyant tobacco auctioneer, intervened and persuaded the mob to merely buy Jordan and his family one-way train tickets out of town. Responding to events in Durham, the *Wilmington Messenger*, owned by an African American, issued a mild reproof:

> Situated as we are in localities of large colored populations at the South, where the least feeling and excitement may at any moment precipitate riot and bloodshed between the hot-headed of both races, the conservators of peace have to be constantly on the alert to prevent the worst consequences.

To that, the *Recorder* huffed:

> The man or writer, white or black, or the newspapers that champion the cause of the fellow Jordon [*sic*] and his secret modes of stirring up strife and embittering the minds of one class against another, or any other white-skinned man like him, is no true friend of peace, order, Durham or the State of North Carolina.

W.T. BLACKWELL. He took over the Bull Durham company after John Green's death, then took in as partner Julian Carr. Blackwell made a fortune in tobacco, then lost everything when his bank failed in 1888. (Courtesy of the Durham County Public Library.)

A decade later, the *Messenger* would be silenced in the Wilmington Race Riot of 1898. Meantime, Durham's attentions had been diverted from the Jordan case by a depression following the failure of W.T. Blackwell's Bank of Durham. The bank took 16 other businesses down with it, along with the personal fortune of Blackwell, who had retired from the Bull in 1883 and was christened in Paul's 1884 *History* as "the father of Durham."

Blackwell never recovered. He spent the last years of his life subsisting largely on the charity of his former competitor Benjamin Duke. After he passed away in 1903, his homeplace on Chapel Hill Street was acquired by a growing congregation. Upon that spot, catty-corner from Ben Duke's Four Acres estate, began rising in 1907 the new sanctuary of Main Street Methodist Church, the church begun in the Duke factory and landed by Brodie Duke. In 1917, it was renamed Duke Memorial.

Blackwell had been a Baptist.

In his Thomas Wolfe-ish novel *American Gold,* Ernest Seeman, of a venerable printing and publishing family in Durham, gave a balloonist's-eye view of "Warham" of the late 1880s:

On the southerly side of the town was a height, with large houses and well-groomed lawns, where several of its richest and most righteous rajputs and masters of machinery lived. Officially, it was McLauchlen's Hill. In popular parlance . . . it was Swelldoodle Hill. And directly below it, in a poverty-struck and stenchful bottom, sprawled a settlement of factory workers' shacks. Down from the Hill ran a nasty little creek. Known to the workers as Sickness Creek. Out of which their children fished medicine bottles, wine bottles. There to the southeast (and also at all the undesirable and disreputable edges, dumping brinks and smelly sewage brooklets) lived the black washerwomen who kept their white betters in clean linen.

In *Proud Shoes*, Pauli Murray described the same section of town as it was in the 1910s:

In 50 years, Durham had spread rapidly from a village to a bustling factory center, sucking in the rolling pine country around it. Shacks for

W.T. BLACKWELL'S RESIDENCE. It stood caty-corner from the Durham home of Ben Duke, whose charity largely supported his aging and bankrupted former competitor. After Blackwell died, his property was acquired for the new sanctuary of Duke Memorial Methodist Church. (Courtesy of Duke Manuscripts Collection.)

factory workers mushroomed in the lowlands between the graded streets. These little communities, which clung precariously to the banks of streams or sat crazily on washed out gullies and were held together by cowpaths or rutted wagon tracks, were called the Bottoms. It was as if the town had swallowed more than it could hold and had regurgitated, for the Bottoms was an odorous conglomeration of trash piles, garbage dumps, cow stalls, pigpens and crowded humanity. And the smell of putrefaction, pig swill, cow dung and frying foods.

One other incident of the 1880s demonstrated Durham's Dodge City heart. This was the "Moonlight Railroad."

In 1871, the North Carolina Railroad had leased its line to the Richmond & Danville, which enjoyed a monopoly on service to towns along the line and treated them accordingly. Even Hiram Paul was moved to complain:

> Railroad facilities are hardly adequate, only one train a day each way being allowed by the liberal policy of the Richmond & Danville system. The depot is a reproach, there being no reception room for either ladies or gentlemen, and the apartment used as such, and adjoining the ticket office, being so filthy and offensive that ladies never apply for tickets, except in cases of absolute necessity. It is to be hoped, however, that the importance of the city will arouse this mammoth monopoly from its complacent lethargy, and that decent facilities at least will soon be afforded.

Arousal was not forthcoming and the city elders set out to make things better. They incorporated and built railroads of their own, first in 1888 with the Durham & Clarksville, which was immediately leased out to the Richmond & Danville. In March 1889, the Durham & Northern was completed, connecting Durham with the Seaboard system at Henderson, North Carolina.

However, there was a logistical problem: the Durham & Northern's terminal property was at Dillard Street, 1 mile east of high-volume Duke cigarette factory. The rival Richmond & Danville refused to share its track, and provided only grudging switching service. Frustrated, the town aldermen in session of April 6 authorized the Durham & Northern to extend its line along Peabody Street, parallel with and just north of the Richmond & Danville, but within the old North Carolina Railroad right of way. Court proceedings loomed, but a band of intrepid townsmen gathered by the light of the moon on April 9 and began laying track westward.

As soon as the sun rose and Richmond & Danville authorities saw what was going on, they called the constabulary and had the workmen arrested for trespassing. Several hours later, town authorities dismissed the charges and the line was finished that night. The next morning, a Richmond & Danville crew began ripping up the Durham & Northern track until townspeople arrived and

NORTH CAROLINA RAILROAD, 1870. Opened in 1855, the line linked a crescent of interior towns with eastern ports and the nation's growing railroad network. (Courtesy of the Duke Manuscripts Collection.)

took up armed guard. Later, the Durham & Northern parked freight cars on the track to block another attack; the Richmond & Danville started building a connecting switch so it could move the cars off.

After two years of litigation, a court ruled that control of the Peabody Street corridor had reverted to the city. In 1895, the Southern Railroad bought the Richmond & Danville, going back to court and making its case by 1903 that the reversion had been voided by the Richmond & Danville's sale. The Seaboard, which had bought the Durham & Northern in 1901, would have to pay rent. While all this was going on in 1899, the Durham & Roxboro was built and opened to a Ramseur Street end-of-the-line, near the site of former Prattsburg, and promptly sold to the Norfolk & Western.

Perhaps the Southern Railroad was still smarting, since in 1904 it announced plans to built a sidetrack down Pettigrew Street on the south side of its right of way. The aldermen quickly passed an ordinance against the track, but the Southern went to work anyway in March 1905 and continued until halted by a state-court injunction. Carrying the matter up to a federal court, the railroad won out on the basis of the 1903 decision, then filed suit against the aldermen for all the trouble they had caused. The suit was tossed out of court.

Meantime, fed up with the trouble, Durham pushed a bill through the state legislature that forced all the railroads serving town to share a single "Union" station. Designed in the Italian Renaissance style with a distinctive square, 65-foot tower and ornate exterior brickwork, and built at the foot of Church Street, the new station opened on May Day of 1905 in a spirit of holiday. A crowd of onlookers gathered to see the first tickets issued and catch the train to Raleigh to watch their Bulls take on the capital's team. The crowd discovered one overlooked detail: there was no mailbox for dispatching the railroad express mail, but they could still take pride in the freshly paved and sidewalked approach to Main Street.

That approach had sparked considerable debate, some feeling it should be rerouted from Church Street so that new arrivals would not have to pass the jail on their way uptown and perhaps get a bad impression. That image problem was solved with a sturdy fence and, within a year, the city was welcoming 26 trains a day.

Union Station served until the railroads discontinued passenger service to Durham in 1965. It was torn down in 1967 to make way for a Downtown Loop road and parking deck. In 1994, just across the tracks from the station site, Durham County opened its new, seven-story, pearly white jailhouse.

THE ITALIANATE TOWER OF UNION STATION. This structure was a landmark in Durham from opening day in 1905 until demolition for urban renewal in 1967. (Courtesy of the Durham County Public Library.)

7. RENOWN

Today, Durham can seem a place unto itself and hardly a part of North Carolina. It is part of a metropolis-in-progress, one of only two in the state. The other is Charlotte, which the rest of North Carolina regards as part of South Carolina for all practical purposes. With its white-collar economy, it no longer shares in the agricultural sensibilities and manufacturing ups and downs that dominate a state of small towns. Along with the whites, African Americans, and Hispanics who typify the state's population, Durham has an appreciable number of Koreans, Indians, and Europeans among its residents. It is not unusual to overhear a conversation in French, Chinese, or Arabic at the grocery store. With multinational businesses and an international university, with citizens who casually fly up to New York for theater weekends, Durham is part of that larger world connected through its generic airports.

A century ago, that was not the case. Durham and its institutions were part and parcel of the social, political, religious, and economic yin and yang of North Carolina, a condition never better encapsulated than in the Bassett Case.

Trinity College arrived at Durham from humble beginnings, but also with a history of ambitious leaders. Founded as a one-room schoolhouse on John Brown's plantation in northern Randolph County near present High Point, c. 1830, its mission of enlightening rustic youth called young Brantley York away from his job in a distillery. York, who aspired to the ministry, took over running the school and in 1839 saw its name changed to Union Institute, recognizing the "union" of Methodist and Quaker interests in education that the school represented

In 1842, York was succeeded by alumnus Braxton Craven, who turned Union into a teacher-training school and secured a state charter as a Normal College. Five years later in 1856, he talked the North Carolina Methodist Convention into supporting the school and so its name changed again to the more pious "Trinity."

Church support or not, the cash flow was erratic, though war and Reconstruction never forced its closure, as they did the University at Chapel Hill. In 1883, the good Methodist Julian S. Carr, riding the crest of Bull Durham's fame, joined the Trinity Board, bringing Durham and its money into the picture just as the school had entered a crisis period upon Craven's death. After muddling

TRINITY COLLEGE. The school was removed from Randolph County to Durham in 1892, and located on the site of a former horse racetrack west of the town, Blackwell Park. (Courtesy of The Herald-Sun *library.)*

through for five years under rule of a three-man committee, of which Carr was a member, Trinity undertook a fund drive that brought in not only $10,000 in Durham Cotton Manufacturing stock, but its first donation from W. Duke Sons & Company.

In 1887, the college brought aboard a 29-year-old Yale man, John Franklin Crowell, as its new president. Already tested in the art of academic management and zealous for progressive education, Crowell figured what Trinity needed was to get out of the sticks. There was opposition. The surrounding village of Trinity depended on the school for its livelihood, professors did not want to move, alumni hated to break with tradition, and the church feared giving up the clean countryside to enter some town of temptations. Nevertheless, the persuasive Yalie prevailed and before the decade turned, even the Methodist Conference had signed onto the idea of "removal."

It proved a happy coincidence, since at just about that time, the burghers of Durham, aware that they had an image problem, set out to buy themselves some class and culture. The state Baptist Convention was looking for a place to build a new women's college. Durham promised twice the local support of any other town, but the good Baptists turned it down, regarding the rough and rum-soaked mill town as no place they would send their daughters.

Insulted when Meredith College took root in Raleigh, the capitalists of Durham took note of Trinity. Crowell made a good impression on Washington Duke when the elder of W. Duke Sons & Company attended a Trinity commencement and, learning that Raleigh had made another nice offer, Duke discreetly let Crowell know that Durham could do better. Ignoring scorn from other quarters of "those cigarette people," Crowell attended on Duke, who proved as good as his word with an $85,000 endowment. Carr chipped in his 62-acre Blackwell Park west of town and lumber from the grandstands at its racetrack would be recycled into the college gym. Other local worthies added $10,000 more and Trinity moved into its new home for the 1892–1893 academic year.

Before its first commencement, depression hit.

The panic of 1893 had effects that reached beyond finance for a state with a long history of poverty, especially for a region still depressed from the war and reviving only as a colonial outpost of the Eastern financial establishment.

Most immediately for Trinity College, the Methodist donations that had been expected to follow Duke's and Carr's lead never came in and the Dukes—father Wash and son Ben both—began to lose their own formerly active interest. The shortfall only aggravated tensions over pay between the college administration, its professors, and trustees. Resentment lingered about the move and Crowell's personality.

The depression also caused problems between the state's denominational colleges such as Trinity, Davidson, and Wake Forest, and its public university, which were all competing for limited supplies of students and money. The denominations had lobbied against reopening the University of North Carolina and the financial antagonism only intensified after the university resumed instruction in 1875. In 1896, the North Carolina Baptist Convention resolved that

TRINITY PRESIDENT JOHN CARLISLE KILGO. He was a fiery advocate for denominational colleges and an abrasive iconoclast, who became a focal point of controversy. (Courtesy of Duke University Archives.)

the state running a school of its own was "unjust to the private and corporate and denominational institutions voluntarily supported," and that it was unfair to tax citizens for a luxury they could not afford to use, while draining money from the already inadequate primary schools.

Complicating the issue was a heated debate over academic liberty, with spokesmen for the colleges claiming that state-controlled teaching and enquiry were not only compromised by political expedience, but taking a sinister turn to the secular, this at the time when literary criticism and Darwinian theory were hauling Christianity's supposed fundamentals into dangerous question. State-school supporters answered that the denominational colleges were beholden to their own benefactors. Trinity, in the 1890s, was tainted by its ties to the "cigarette people" and their "blood money." Tobacco was fundamental to North Carolina's economy, but the corporations that turned it into fortunes were regarded with suspicion at best and often with outright hostility. Buck Duke's American Tobacco conglomerate was accused of forcing prices down and keeping farmers in a condition of practical serfdom.

Not only that, but in the Gay 1890s and 1900s, the United States was on one of its periodic health kicks and, even in the Old North State, there was widespread opposition to the growing, selling, and using of tobacco products. When temperance crusader Carrie Nation paid a call on Durham in 1907, the cigarette factories were more targets of her wrath than the saloons. Already, righteousness had brought a bill before the North Carolina legislature to ban the sale of cigarettes and rolling papers. (It did not pass.)

Into this mix came John Carlisle Kilgo, a fiery and abrasive iconoclast whom Trinity's trustees made their president upon Crowell's resignation in 1894. Kilgo was an outspoken champion of Christian schools and firmly aligned himself and the college with the Republican, monopoly-making Duke family.

Meantime, farmers across the South were signing onto the Populist movement that had begun in Texas in the 1870s and swept east and north as commodity prices fell and freight rates and fertilizer prices went up. Populists were for government regulation of commerce and against the gold standard and big business. That meant they were against the industrializing fundamentals of the New South and against the Southern Democrats, whose economic interests matched those of the Northern Republicans. Populist thinking was leading poor whites and poor African Americans to acknowledge that they had issues and interests in common, and what was left of Southern Republicanism was ready to take them in.

In North Carolina, home of the famed and powerful Populist Leonidas Polk, "Fusionists," Populist-minded activists who allied with either disaffected Democrats or Republicans, as suited their agendas, swept into power in the wake of the 1893 crash. For them, it was like 1868 all over again, an opportunity to go back and finish creating the new, biracial civilization Reconstruction had begun and Redemption had stonewalled. For the Democrats, this was it. Dealing the race card, raising the specter of "Negro domination," race mixing, and dispatching red-shirted storm troopers to dispense Ku Klux–style thuggery, the Democrats regained power in the elections of 1898 and 1900. They then set about consolidating their authority once and for all, with voting restraints and divided public accommodations codified into the law.

Of course the trusts were right up there too, as a prod for rousing emotions and riling the troops. They sometimes offered themselves with racial coloring as a package to the Democrats, as when the Dukes' college invited black educator Booker T. Washington to speak on campus while he was in Durham for the 1896 Colored County Fair.

Up for re-election in 1900, George White, an African-American congressman from North Carolina's eastern "Black Second" district, realized there was no point in running. White would be the last African American to serve in Congress for 25 years and the last from the South until after the Civil Rights Movement. He resolved to leave the state, saying, "I cannot live in North Carolina and be a man. I do not believe the black man has much relief in any political party. He must paddle his own canoe. He must think for himself and act for himself. Legislation will not help him."

Through all the turbulence, Durham's growing black community had been doing just that. Richard Fitzgerald had an 18-room Queen Anne home in a grove of shade trees just west of town. Old-timers in the Burch Avenue-Gattis Street neighborhood point out the nearby gullies as remains of Fitzgerald's clay pits. (That neighborhood would produce a tycoon of its own, international highway contractor Nello Teer, who was born on Burch Avenue in 1888.) Brother Robert, who had split off on his own, saw his brick business falter along with his war-injured eyesight. His home was modest, on a slope between the town cemetery and one of the Bottoms, but he called his place "Homestead on the Hillside" and carried himself proud, tall, and every inch a soldier.

Richard had taken his brick profits and diversified, just like his white counterparts in Durham. He was a founder of Mechanics and Farmers Bank and had interests in drugstores, cotton mills, and tobacco. There were others like him. John Merrick, trained as a bricklayer under slavery, came to Raleigh after Emancipation to work on the freedmen's Shaw University. He then became shoeshine man in a barber shop, learned the haircutting trade, and moved over to the opportunity-filled town of Durham.

Bull City tradition has long maintained that it was one of the tycoons— Washington Duke, Julian Carr, or W.T. Blackwell—or all three who suggested Merrick's move, feeling their town had risen to a point where its leading citizens should not have to go away for a good shave and trim. More likely, it was a competing barber in Raleigh, or Merrick may well have come up with the idea on his own. In any event, he opened a shop in 1882 and a decade later owned a chain of two shops for African Americans and three for whites, advertising the latter as having everything sterilized, "even the Negro."

Regular client Washington Duke, apparently conscious of his appearance, took Merrick along on business trips to New York. Exposed to and probably inspired by what money could be used to do, Merrick branched out into real estate and residential construction, along with insurance. That last enterprise culminated in formation of the North Carolina Mutual and Provident Association in 1898. With partners C.C. Spaulding and Aaron Moore, a physician, Merrick moved the Mutual in 1905 to a new building all its own on Parrish Street in the heart of Durham's uptown business district, aided by the banks owned by George Watts and Ben Duke.

Watts's and Duke's patronage had already been diverted to a community need across the tracks. The hospital Watts gave Durham in 1895 was for whites only, although by 1900 he was thinking of adding an African-American wing. Dr. Aaron Moore, however, convinced Watts that black physicians needed a hospital of their own. About this time, the Duke brothers approached some prominent black citizens with the proposition to erect a memorial in honor of the loyal slaves who looked after the Confederacy's womenfolk while their men were off to the War. In essence, the reply was, "That's a real nice idea, but what we could use is a hospital."

So, with Duke financing, Lincoln Hospital opened in 1901 with a plaque in its lobby reading:

GEORGE WHITE, UNITED STATES CONGRESSMAN. White was from North Carolina's "Black Second" district, and left the state after elections in 1898 and 1900 gave the Democratic party a race-based lock on political power. (Courtesy of North Carolina Division of Archives and History.)

MEMORIAM
LINCOLN   1901   HOSPITAL
With grateful appreciation and loving remembrance of the
fidelity and faithfulness of the Negro slaves to the Mothers
and Daughters of the Confederacy, during the Civil War,
this institution was founded by one of the Fathers and Sons
B.N. Duke J.B. Duke W. Duke
Not one act of disloyalty was recorded against them.
JOHN MERRICK, President
A.M. Moore, Founder and Supt.

After Lincoln Hospital was torn down in 1983, the plaque and other memorabilia went into a waiting-room display at Durham Regional Hospital, a product of the final merger of black and white institutions.

Back in the 1910s, the Mutual spun off Mechanics and Farmers Bank, then the Merrick-Moore-Spaulding Land Company The triumvirate's associates, in various combinations for various businesses, included insurance man Richard Fitzgerald, educator W.G. Pearson, pharmacist J.A. Dodson, and a young fellow in the loan and investment business named James Shepard.

Shepard came to Durham from Raleigh when his father became pastor at White Rock Church. Educated as a pharmacist, holding two degrees from Shaw University, he co-founded the Durham Drug Company, but even as he increased in business he felt a call to greater opportunity. Speaking at the Piedmont Colored Fair in Charlotte in 1903, Shepard had a reply for former Congressman White:

> The apostle Paul, when beset on all sides by men who would destroy him, exclaimed, "I am a Roman citizen," and these words, like magic, threw around him the protection of the law. My mind reverts to these scenes today, as on every side I see progress. It makes me proud of the fact that I am an American citizen.
>
> With no long line of traceable descent, no heraldry, no glory nor pomp of power, still I can join with the dominant race and say that I, too, am an American citizen.

Before long, he would hear the call to start a college.

Meanwhile, back at the Trinity campus, all the existing conflicts had been joined by one within the Methodist Church. John Carlisle Kilgo was in a feud with trustee Walter Clark over various matters, including Kilgo's opposition to state-supported colleges, his closeness to the Dukes, his support for faculty tenure, and his general unorthodoxy where conservative, Democratic attitudes were concerned. Their bad blood coalesced into a lengthy lawsuit in which Thomas J. Gattis, a Methodist minister angry over his forced retirement, claimed he had been slandered by Kilgo. Kilgo and his supporters, in turn, thought Gattis had been feeding Clark information with which Clark could slander Kilgo. The case was, in time, dismissed, but not before its two sides had their say in the popular press and the church's major patrons divided according to which side they were on.

Then along came Bassett.

John Spencer Bassett, who was recording so much of Durham's interesting history, was a Southerner indignant over the turn his country's politics and thinking had taken toward intolerance, orthodoxy, and believing its own deceits. Hoping to rouse fellow intellectuals into an opposition force, he started an academic journal, the *South Atlantic Quarterly*, and in its October 1903 issue, he published his own attack on those he held to be "Stirring Up the Fires of Race Antipathy."

Fighting words enough, but in the essay Bassett stated that Booker T. Washington was the second-greatest man born in the South in the last 100 years. Having not wholly taken leave of his sense of self-preservation, Bassett did allow that the first was General Robert E. Lee.

Setting the tone for the hue and cry that rose for Bassett's head, or at least his job, was Raleigh publisher Josephus Daniels, who had bought that city's *News and Observer* in 1894 and made it, for all practical purposes, a house organ for the state's Democratic establishment. Already in 1898 the "Old Reliable" had reported that James B. Duke's American Tobacco Trust had attempted an alliance with the Populists of Durham County. In April 1901, it stated that "Duke

DURHAM'S PUBLIC LIBRARY. The first in North Carolina, the library occupied a house at Five Points in 1898, product of a town-gown effort led by Trinity professor Edwin Mims and Lallah Ruth Carr, daughter of tobacco tycoon Julian Carr. (Courtesy of Durham County Public Library.)

PRESIDENT THEODORE ROOSEVELT. Roosevelt spoke from a flatcar, attended by Trinity College and Durham dignitaries, many of whom must have felt both deferential and embarrassed at what the Republican president had to say. (Courtesy of Duke University Archives.)

cigarettes destroy mind and body at home and give us a bad name abroad," quoting a missionary who had seen Durham-made cigarettes for sale in China, their packages decorated with pictures of nude women.

(Buck Duke, no slouch in the marketing department himself, had trumped the Bull's premiums by including picture cards of attractive women, sometimes in scanty clothing, in packs of his cigarettes. His father objected, but the gimmick worked.)

In September 1901, a *News and Observer* article suggested that Leon Czolgosz, assassin of President McKinley, had been depraved by immoderate smoking. Once the statement of "bASSett"—Daniels's spelling—came out, the Raleigh paper was on the attack, echoed by a host of fellow traveling editors and encouraged by the successful effort the year before in Georgia to roust an offensive professor of Emory University.

Outside of North Carolina, though, Trinity graduates and friends were sending messages of support for Kilgo to hold the line for intellectual freedom. Walter Hines Page wrote to Ben Duke, saying that Bassett must not be "driven out on the cry of 'nigger.' " In the end, which came in the wee hours of December 2 at a meeting especially called for the occasion, the college trustees voted 12 to 7 to let Bassett remain on the payroll. Students, listening at the door for any word they could catch, whooped. They bolted for the athletic field, cheered, and burned Josephus Daniels in effigy. The next week, the *Wilkesboro Chronicle* was sniffling about "the cigarette smart alecks."

Secured in his position, Bassett built himself a new, Southern-columned home just across the street from campus. It could only have been with quiet satisfaction that Kilgo and his supporters heard the congratulations of President Theodore Roosevelt, Republican, spoken from a Persian-carpeted flatcar just outside the Trinity gate in October 1905. The other side could but squirm in embarrassed, perfunctory politeness. It was, however, a passing moment. Bassett would eventually leave and finish out his career at Smith College in Massachusetts. Jim Crow law and dogma would rule in the South for half a century, John Kilgo would become a bishop of the Methodist Church in 1910, and Trinity College would have a new leader, a descendant of that William Few who had hit the road to Georgia so very long ago.

James Shepard by that time had thrown himself into missionary work, traveling to Africa and Europe and addressing an international Sunday school conference in Rome. In 1908, he began working on ideas for a school of his own, similar to the Northfield Bible Training School that evangelist D.L. Moody had founded in the Berkshire wilds of western Massachusetts. Shepard's school would teach foreign languages and medicine along with the Bible, for workers called to foreign vineyards. His idea found support in Durham, including that of the *Recorder*: "Dr. James E. Shepard has been at work on the plan for some time, and that his efforts are in a measure successful is cause for all members of the colored race in Durham and their white friends to rejoice."

Shepard organized a money-raising group in March 1909, and received 20 acres on Fayetteville Street from Brodie Duke. By summer, plans included Bible classes for men and women, a department to teach illiterate preachers to read, a course for Sunday school teachers, a YMCA training program, and classes in agriculture, "domestic science," and other "practical industries." By fall, with Merrick, Moore, and Pearson assisting, along with the Durham Merchants' Association, Shepard had $25,000 in hand; a name, the National Religious Training School and Chautauqua; and officers. He would be president, Moore was secretary, and treasurer would be Julian Carr, by now a "General of Confederate veterans."

School started in July of 1910.

Booker Washington visited Durham again in 1910. At stop after stop before he arrived, he was told, "Wait 'til you get to Durham." Washington was not disappointed, finding the Mutual, Mechanics and Farmers and the Bull City Drug Company (one of the first uses of the term "Bull City") all uptown, two textile factories, and houses spread across Hayti, all operated and owned by African Americans. The man from Tuskegee praised the progress of black Durham, the leadership of Merrick and his associates, and the philanthropies and enlightened hiring practices of Carr and Duke.

In 1911, Durham was paid a call by the militant African-American intellectual W.E.B. DuBois, who was similarly impressed:

> Durham has not feared. It has distinctly encouraged the best type of
> black man by active aid and passive tolerance . . . To-day there is a

singular group in Durham where a black man may get up in the morning from a mattress made by black men, in a house which a black man built out of lumber which black men cut and planed; he may put on a suit which he bought at a colored haberdashery and socks knit at a colored mill; he may cook victuals from a colored grocery on a stove which black men fashioned; he may earn his living working for colored men, be sick in a colored hospital, and buried from a colored church; and the Negro insurance society will pay his widow enough to keep his children in a colored school. This is surely progress.

By 1910, Durham had a population of 18,000 and had extended its limits to form a rectangle of more than 4 square miles, still centered on the depot. It had an amusement park, Lakewood, at the southwest end of the streetcar line, and suburbs growing wherever the trolleys reached. It had a public library, the first in North Carolina, opened in a house at Five Points on February 1, 1898, the product of a town-and-gown collaboration led by Trinity professor Edwin Mims and Lallah Ruth Carr, the General's daughter. It was home to the Southern Conservatory of Music, founded the same year as the library by professor Gilmore Ward Bryant.

There was a chamber of commerce and a rival, the Commonwealth Club, which were headed, respectively, by E.J. Parrish and Julian Carr, brothers-in-law whose relations were still strained from Carr's foreclosing on Parrish during the Panic of 1893. Business was business. There were a golf club, driving club, cotillion club, art club, and a chapter of the Daughters of the American Revolution was not far away.

For some time, there had been public schools for the segregated races, establishment of which had brought an unusual play of the old race card.

In 1881, soon after Durham County was created, the legislature provided for Durham County to vote whether to tax itself for a public graded school. Local sentiments were not overwhelmingly favorable, since it seemed unfair to tax everybody to pay for something that some people could afford on their own. Several existing private schools had no need for competition, anyway. The anti–faction thought it found a key objection, and brought to light the provision that white tax dollars would go to pay for a white school, black dollars for a black. Since there were so many fewer black taxpayers, any schools so funded would be inevitably un-equal and grossly unfair. Their broadside stated the following:

> We of Durham, have always professed to do full justice to the colored people, and in fact went so far as to elect the chief white Republican of the county [Wash Duke] Commissioner for the county, in consideration of the solid vote given by [black citizens] to support the new county.

It was an imaginative ploy, but it did not work. The referendum passed in May 1882. A Durham Graded School Committee, representing both town and county,

THE DURHAM GRADED SCHOOL. This picture shows pupils and faculty outside the school, which opened in the Main Street Wright's Factory (the white building) on September 4, 1882. (Courtesy of Durham Public Library.)

was created. Professor E.W. Kennedy of Goldsboro was hired as superintendent and on September 4, school opened in a frame building called Wright's Factory on Main Street near the Duke factory. Enrollment was 308 that first year.

By 1885 the school had nine grades in all and added faculty and needed more money, which meant higher taxes. Founding father Atlas Rigsbee, owner of the Durham Female Seminary, went to court for a restraining order. Turned down by the aforementioned Judge Walter Clark, Rigsbee took his case to the state supreme court, which declared the original law authorizing Durham's public school was unconstitutional, due to its discriminatory funding provision.

With the school facing bankruptcy, W.T. Blackwell, whose own lending habits were still three years away from bankrupting him, offered to cover its cost until a new, legal law could be enacted and taxes levied again. His offer inspired several others to share the burden, so the school was saved and put on firm legal ground in 1887 after some voting irregularities were cleared up. That same year a new, brick school was opened for Durham's African-American children, whose education had been privately undertaken while the courts and litigants were too busy to interfere.

By 1887, Durham even had two distinct and dueling factory whistles, as Duke had introduced a war whoop to counter the Bull's bellow. If Trinity won a ballgame, the Indian would scream. If the University of North Carolina won one, the Bull let go. Either could be taken as a sound of triumph, as the *Tobacco Plant* exulted upon the victory for education: "As long as Blackwell's Bull growls out his welcome to the moon, as long as Duke's warhoop scares the sun away from the evening sky, as long as tobacco grows and smoke curls upward, the graded schools of Durham will go on with increasing usefulness and popularity."

December 15, 1913: Monday night at Christmastime and a crowd estimated generously and in retrospect at 10,000 collected in downtown Durham.

Excitement had been fed for weeks, the railroads advertising special trains into the city from such outlying points as Roxboro, Oxford, and Raleigh, the merchants plugging Christmas sales. The focal point of it all was a rickety metal framework perched atop the Wright Building at Church and Main with a fine exposure toward the Union Station.

By day, that is, it appeared a rickety metal framework. Once darkness fell, the contraption would be transformed into a glowing beacon of electrical magic, with 1,230 red, green, amber, and white bulbs proclaiming:

DURHAM
RENOWNED
THE WORLD AROUND
HEALTH SUCCESS WEALTH PROGRESS

to the tune of 5,500 candlepower.

THE SLOGAN SIGN. Erected atop a downtown building and lit up before a Christmastime crowd on December 15, 1913, it was a gift from the Durham Traction Company.

The Slogan Sign was a gift from the Durham Traction Company, which had been on a vigorous campaign to sell merchants on electric signs and illuminated displays. Joining in the planning with verve and vigor was the new Commercial Club, which made promises recounted by a newspaper report:

> . . . to give Durham, for the holiday season at least, one of the brightest and prettiest business streets ever planned to arouse the holiday spirits of the shoppers.
>
> We feel safe in saying without fear of successful contradiction or charge of boasting that Durham will be the first and only real "man size" electrically lighted slogan sign in North Carolina.

There was nothing to compare, the city was assured by those who should know, any closer than Montgomery, Alabama.

W.G. Bramham, one in a succession of speakers helping build the anticipation that chilly evening, compared the Slogan Sign, blazing forth from the town of 20,000, to Nelson's proclamation at Trafalgar that "England expects every man to do his duty!" to "The sword of the Lord and Gideon!" that dazzled the Midianites in the Book of Judges, and to the "Brilliant light in the form of a star, which advertised and proclaimed to the wise men of the east the greatest event of all time."

Costumed citizens held a "tacky parade," with the top prize, a $10 Aetna accident insurance policy, going to Logan Weldon. Miss Annie Laura Beaman, a beautiful brunette, decorated a float with a horse-and-buggy theme devised by the Durham Vehicle and Harness Company. The East Durham and Trinity College bands made music. Santa Claus dropped by.

The speakers droned on—R.L. Lindsey of the Traction Company, S.C. Chambers and Branham of the Commercial Club, Mayor W.J. Brogden—but no one beyond the immediate vicinity of the speakers' stand could hear them. There were inopportune cheers and blowing of horns, streetcars rang their bells, trying to move spectators off their tracks, one person and another shouted for everyone else to be quiet, and a cab driver shooed off a kid who had taken a vantage point atop a new, $7 fender.

Then the time had come. Mayor Brogden flipped the switch. A shimmering red and amber border appeared. Then "Renowned The World Around," then "Health," "Wealth," "Progress," "Success."

No "Durham."

Dignitaries on the stand squirmed. Citizens in the streets hooted. Electrons in the wiring took their time. After a long, anxious, and awkward pause, "Durham" did come out, as if stage-frighted, bashful, or downright embarrassed.

8. Transition Times

On Sunday, June 20, 1926, the *Durham Sun* carried a half-page photo spread on one of Durham's best-known residents. The headline read, "Jerry Markham's Life Is Unique."

The spread itself was unique, too. Jerry Markham was African American.

Not only that, but Jerry Markham was no master of merchandising, no executive of insurance, no preacher. He was the crossing guard on Duke Street. In community estimation, however, he was a philosopher.

"No king on his throne gets more real enjoyment in his modern convenience palace than I do in my home," he would tell anyone who would listen. That home was a 9-foot by 15-foot shanty beside the Southern Railroad track, just up from the old Duke tobacco complex—now belonging to Liggett & Myers, since the Supreme Court had busted Buck Duke's trust in 1911—and down from the mansion district on Chapel Hill Street.

The day the photographer came, Sarah Duke was paying a neighborly call down from her Four Acres. She posed with Markham outside his residence, looking uncomfortably at the camera among his pecking chickens, while Markham grinned at her.

Around his shack, with its brick chimney, Markham tended peach trees and a lush patch of greens. Inside, a man to take care of his own business, Markham stored his coffin. Above it all, he flew the Confederate national flag. He never married. Once asked about that, he said, "I'd rather have a cow. A cow doesn't talk back to you like a woman does."

Markham, like his adopted hometown, was a combination of hard sense and eccentricity. The press first took note of him in 1913 when he appeared at the Driver Street ballpark, another attraction at the end of a streetcar line, to cheer the Durham Bulls, decked out in top hat and tails. On game days, he would walk through downtown taking a pep rally wherever he went. When the team played out of town, Markham went along, mascot and cheerleader. Once, in Raleigh, he so antagonized the home crowd that they pelted him with eggs. Raleigh fans were looking for him when the teams next played in Durham and Markham declared that not every man (nor, presumably, every egg) of the capital could keep him away from the game.

At the same time, Markham gave away his surplus produce and extra milk from his cow, a gift from Ben Duke which, Markham said, produced six quarts a day. He was also quietly acquiring real estate, perhaps $10,000 worth (about a quarter-million dollars by today's measure) and accounts whose balances he kept strictly between himself and his bankers.

That Sunday feature—which, sad to say, survives only in a crude photocopy in the late *Sun* columnist Wyatt Dixon's book *How Times Do Change*—itself presents a quick study of Durham in the 1920s: the flag, the shanty, a horse to one side, and the solid tobacco buildings for a backdrop; society matron and former retainer of similar age; and Markham beside his own tombstone, already set on the plot he had bought and inscribed with his chosen epitaph for an era going by:

"An old slave and a friend to all."

Markham, in 1926, had some years ahead, but not so for many of the builders of a town now grown and expanded to almost 44,000. The Slogan Sign had not made it to the Roaring Twenties, falling victim to a windstorm and declared by the chamber of commerce in 1919 to not be worth the cost of repair. Richard Fitzgerald died in 1918, followed the next year by his brother Robert, John Merrick, and Brodie Duke. E.J. Parrish, the auctioneer and rescuer of Radical blacksmith E.G. Jordan, passed in 1920; George Watts in 1921; Dr. Aaron Moore in 1923.

SARAH DUKE AND JERRY MARKHAM, 1926. Railroad crossing guard and philosopher Markham gets a visit from neighbor Mrs. Ben Duke at his home beside the railroad tracks. (Courtesy of Duke Manuscripts Collection, B.N. Duke Papers.)

DEDICATION CEREMONY FOR THE UNITY MONUMENT AT BENNETT PLACE, NOVEMBER 8, 1923. White-haired "General" Julian Carr is seen dozing off at right. (Courtesy of Durham County Public Library.)

Durham lost its General, Julian S. Carr, in 1924. Southgate Jones Sr. remembers in his memoir:

> General Carr was probably the most exquisitely groomed gentleman in North Carolina, usually attired in a black broadcloth cutaway coat, silk vest, striped trousers, a colorful tie, and never without a white carnation in his lapel. These were perfect complements for his alert blue eyes, his florid complexion, his carefully clipped gray mustache.

Carr was a man of contrasting natures: impatient, generous, reactionary, imaginative, spiritual, tough. He saw to it that a marker was placed upon every Confederate grave in Maplewood Cemetery, he built a cotton mill to be run entirely by African Americans. Tradition says that they were his relatives, including a half-brother from Chapel Hill. The General, too, was a man to keep close watch on his business. At his First National Bank, where Jones observed Carr in action from his youthful post as an assistant teller, Carr personally reviewed each loan as it came up for renewal to decide whose was good and whose time had come to pay up. His decisions were law, sometimes requiring the finest exercise of tact to manipulate in a debtor's favor.

For example, take the case of one George Lyon, traveling salesman for an ammunition company, which Jones observed and recorded for posterity. Lyon was an honest man, but got behind on his payments when he went on long business trips out of town. Summoned to the bank, he strode into the General's office, exclaiming, "General, I certainly am glad to see you! I don't believe I've had the pleasure of shaking your hand in six months." Then, after complimenting Carr's necktie, which he said was like nothing he had seen in all his travels, Lyon himself brought up the business of the notes. Flush with flattery, Carr dismissed the matter: "Renew them as you like. Just tell Southgate to take care of them."

Carr lost his wife Nannie in 1915. Evenings thereafter, a story goes, he would leave the bank and ride the streetcar to Maplewood Cemetery where carved angels watched over her grave. There the General would sit awhile, reading the newspaper aloud to her. "Society pages," one wit commented years later.

Carr lived to see a memorial raised of a different kind. Old timers' war stories had been of little interest to the go-getters of the New South, a condition the veterans lamented as they felt themselves aging: "The new generation hardly comprehends us," said Georgian Paul Hamilton Hayne in 1893. Texan J.B. Beck sadly added, "I know, however, the hard and faithful pull that is necessary to ever arouse the public mind [to listen] to the quivering voice of the old ex-Confederate soldier."

Bennett Place, that momentous farmstead, was abandoned and decaying. Brodie Duke bought it in 1890 with the idea of building a protective wooden shell and then of selling it as a historical curiosity at the Chicago Exposition of 1893.

BENNETT PLACE. Abandoned by the 1890s, this surrender site of the Civil War fell into disrepair and finally burned in 1921. Brodie Duke had once bought the farm, thinking of erecting a protective dome over it. (Courtesy of North Carolina Division of Archives and History.)

There were no takers, so Brodie unloaded the property in 1908 to plantation owner Samuel Morgan. The old house burned in 1921, just as the chamber of commerce undertook a campaign to place a memorial beside it. Persevering, Durham representatives R.O. Everett and Frank Fuller won a pledge of $50 a year from the state to maintain the site. Morgan's heirs donated the land and paid for a monument—twin pillars, capped by a lintel with the word "Unity" inscribed. Over some opposition from the United Daughters of the Confederacy, the monument was raised and dedicated on November 8, 1923. In a photograph of the ceremony, General Carr may be seen dozing while a lone African American man looks on in the foreground.

Durham County took over Bennett Place in 1925. The burned cabins were rebuilt for the Civil War centennial in the 1960s and North Carolina formally adopted them for a state historic site a decade later.

Julian Carr did not live to see his old rival raise a monument of a different kind.

William Preston Few, Kilgo's successor at the helm of Trinity College and descendant of the Regulators, realized that James B. Duke, who had shed his United States tobacco business after the Supreme Court decision and moved on to make more money in hydroelectric power, was getting along in years and might be inclined to leave a worthy testimonial to all he and his family had done. With patient and gentle persuasion, Few led Duke to make the college the primary object of his benevolence. As the academic year of 1924–1925 began, he could tantalizingly announce, "Never before have all indications pointed toward a more promising year."

Rumors had been flying for several years, but few besides Few realized the scale of that promise. On December 9, the facts came out: Buck Duke was going to establish an endowment of $40 million, with 32 percent of the proceeds going to Trinity College on the small condition that it assume the name of "Duke" in honor of old Wash. The patriarch's statue was already watching over the college gate and waiting, the saying still goes, to stand up should ever a virgin pass by.

Needless to say, Trinity's trustees hesitated not a bit to meet Duke's condition and soon began the rebuilding of Trinity's campus and construction of a whole new campus on the old Rigsbee farm a mile to the west—thus outfoxing the speculators who had been snapping up options near the existing college. A flurry of building was already going on downtown. The old Academy of Music on Chapel Hill Street, between Market and Corcoran, which had housed a concert hall and municipal offices above an open-air meat market, was torn down and in its place erected the 16-story Washington Duke Hotel. The old Durham High School on Morris Street became the first city hall, while adjacent to its rear went up the magnificent, 1,400-seat Durham Auditorium, soon to become better known as the Carolina Theatre.

Designed for vaudeville, the auditorium would quickly be converted to a movie house as talkies helped film supplant live shows. Durham had already provided its bit for the entertainment business. Vaudeville comics Charles Correll and Freeman Gosden had met in town in 1920, later teaming up to form the radio duo

DURHAM'S PROFESSIONAL BASEBALL TEAM. This 1913 team photo shows the players with their namesake Durham Bull. (Courtesy of the Durham Bulls.)

Amos 'n' Andy. A two-reel comedy, *Durham's Hero*, had amused townsfolk by its screening as well as its filming among the neighborhoods and streets of the city.

A new baseball field, El Toro Park, went into a bottom just down Morris Street from the city hall in 1926, following the new, Greek revival library on East Main. The Kiwanis Club gave a bookmobile, Miss Kiwanis, in 1923, and civic interests formed a playground commission in 1924, moving the city to create a recreation department. Women liberated by the vote and by activity outside the home during World War I, took up causes of general welfare leading to improved health services, though their investigation of labor conditions in Durham's mills was gently diverted by managers' initiatives on the workers' behalf. Carr allowed his hired help to have some say in management, while William Erwin added an auditorium and park to the Episcopal Church he had already built for his employees' enjoyment. (Not that many mill hands became dedicated Episcopalians.) Erwin's amenities even included a small zoo, which gave the name "Monkey Bottom" to the old Pinhook lowland.

With success following upon success (at least, from the point of view of Durham's elders) the idea dawned that the city should have a pedigree. The chamber of commerce commissioned the Duke historian Kenneth Boyd to research and write a fitting history and it was decided that Dr. Bartlett Durham should have a place of honor in the town that bore his name.

In 1933, the good doctor's body was exhumed from its place among the Snipeses. He was found to be in a remarkable state of preservation, having been buried during a severe freeze. However, diggers cracked a glass plate over his face, releasing a horrifically smelly whiff of embalming fluids that took days in the washpots to get out of spectators' clothing. Dr. Durham was displayed at rural Antioch Church, then in state at Durham's Hall-Wynne Funeral Home, where he was stored for several more months before ceremonial re-interment at Maplewood in early 1934.

While prospects were bullish for Trinity/Duke, across the tracks, James Shepard's Training School had fallen upon hard times. Money remained hard to come by, much less secure, until the state of North Carolina stepped in in 1923. The state took over responsibility and renamed it first the Durham State Normal School and then North Carolina College for Negroes, the first state-supported, liberal arts college for African Americans in the United States. Shepard did, though, remain president.

Ostensibly settled, race relations were still tense in Durham and across the South. The Ku Klux Klan was revived in 1915, inspired by the movie *Birth of a Nation*, set in the South during the Civil War and Reconstruction and depicting the freedmen and their Northern friends as scoundrels, rapists, and worse. President Woodrow Wilson, Southern-born but Princeton affected, watched the picture in the first-ever White House screening and declared it "history writ by lightning." *Birth of a Nation* was based on the novel *The Clansman* by North

JAMES SHEPARD. Pharmacist turned missionary, Shepard founded the National Religious Training School and Chautauqua in Durham in 1910. Taken over by the state of North Carolina in the 1920s, it was the first state-supported liberal arts college for blacks in the United States. (Courtesy of Duke Manuscripts Collection.)

Carolinian Thomas Dixon, a friend of the Durham County Camerons on whom he based a family of genteel Old Southern characters. When the movie was shown in Durham, African-American citizens protested. The last legal hangings in Durham had taken place in 1907—a white man and a black man on the same day—but in 1920 there were a pair of lynchings, one victim an employee of prominent builder Nello Teer who proclaimed the incident "a ghastly mistake."

Beneath the veneer of segregation, black activism went on. In March 1933, Thomas Hocutt, a graduate of North Carolina College, applied for admission to the University of North Carolina's pharmacy school, perhaps the first challenge to the doctrine of separate-but-equal as applied to higher education. "Negro liberals," including attorney William Hastie of the National Association for the Advancement of Colored People, lined up on Hocutt's behalf, but his application was scuttled when Shepard, afraid of alienating the white support on which his school depended, neglected to send the University of North Carolina a copy of Hocutt's transcript.

Shepard's political sensitivity paid off. In 1938, the Supreme Court ordered states to either admit blacks to white universities or provide equivalent professional training at their African American schools. North Carolina College soon got a school of law.

Duke had a school of medicine. Decreed in Duke's indenture, the medical school fulfilled a Durham dream that went back at least 40 years. Speaking at the dedication of Watts Hospital on February 21, 1895, businessman and politician H.A. Foushee looked ahead 50 years to 1945, when a great crowd would be gathered for the opening of "the greatest medical university of the South." Foushee further predicted that, by 1945, the University of North Carolina would be in eastern Durham, "removed from its present situation, in the back woods, and come out into civilization."

A medical department at Trinity College had been an ambition of President Crowell even before the school relocated to Durham, but state disinterest and the economic depression squelched the idea. Later, John Sprunt Hill, George Watts's son-in-law and a University of North Carolina trustee, floated the idea of establishing a state medical school in Durham, working in conjunction with Trinity and Watts Hospital. Institutional turf protection put an end to that.

But with the Duke Endowment, and more of Duke's fortune coming the university's way upon James B. Duke's death in 1925, President Few and associates set out to get their medical school at last. They hired Dr. W.C. Davison of Johns Hopkins to build an up-to-date, innovative hospital and school along the Hopkins model. Indeed, as spreading Depression invaded the nation's ivory towers in the early 1930s, Duke could afford to snap up the best and brightest academic talent that money could buy. As fate would have it, among those talents were J.B. and Louisa Rhine.

Originally inclined to ministry, J.B. Rhine came from a region of Pennsylvania where belief was strong in omens and warnings from powers unseen. His interest in such ethereal forces found spiritual kinship with Louisa Weckesser, whom he

PARAPSYCHOLOGISTS J.B. AND LOUISA RHINE (CENTER). The pair conduct an experiment with two Duke University students. Rhine's pioneering work in what he called "Extra-Sensory Perception" brought unexpected fame to Duke University in the 1930s. (Courtesy of Duke University Archives.)

followed to the University of Chicago after Marine service in World War I. At Chicago, they earned degrees in botany, left to teach at West Virginia, and then heard a talk on spiritualism by the British novelist Sir Arthur Conan Doyle. Old flames stirred. They went to Cambridge to see William McDougall, a psychologist who shared their interest and who, it happened, had just been hired away from Harvard by Duke. McDougall invited the Rhines to come along to Durham in 1927.

In 1932, Duke bestowed a Ph.D. upon one John F. Thomas, whose dissertation was on the novel field of "parapsychology."

J.B. Rhine, with his wife's enthusiastic and well-informed assistance, had been busy turning superstition into science. With a set of cards designed by chemist colleague Carl Zener, he conducted experiments in thought transference, or "mental telepathy," and by 1934 felt he had data substantive enough for publication. His first paper, "Extra-Sensory Perception," reached beyond academic psychology to the popular press where it made a sensation. *Harper's Bazaar* and *American* magazines ran features in 1936 and, in 1937, he issued a book, *New Frontiers of the Mind.* It was snapped up by the Book of the Month Club and led to a nationwide, prime-time radio program. Less than 10 years after its new, Gothic West Campus opened, mind-reading had put Duke University on the international map.

Rhine was not the only resident of Durham heard over America's airwaves. Actually, he was beaten to them by Jerry Markham.

In 1936, W.K. Lipscomb, owner of a Durham clothing business, arranged for Markham to go to New York for NBC's *We the People* show, where he would add commentary to a radio play telling his life story. The homespun African-American philosopher, former slave, former coachman to Washington Duke, ever alert to keep children on their way to school and out of the path of coming trains, and unlucky dealer in bootleg whiskey (he spent a bundle on lawyers and court costs after being caught at the business) rode north in private quarters, thus avoiding any awkwardness about keeping to his "place" on the train, and settled into a room at the YMCA.

Markham told reporters he liked radio host Philip "Boss" Lord, but the big city let him down. Taken to see Wall Street on a Sunday, he felt he missed seeing the money that would have been at work during weekday hours. In the view from a skyscraper, he only saw more buildings. The price of New York coal was too high for his liking. As a touch of home, he carried along his Confederate flag, which provoked questions to which Markham naturally had answers.

In 1861, he told the city press, he wanted to go to war with his master, but his master thought 12 was too young and told the youngster he could serve by flying the Southern flag:

> My old master said to keep that flag up, and nobody will ever take it down as long as I live.
>
> I used to be a slave, but you folks up here are the real slaves, especially to the [factory] whistle. You can't call a minute your own. You have to trust everybody. Me, I buy all my goods in Durham and Mr. Fuller is my lawyer. I trust them and not many other people.

He did allow that, if he should ever live in New York, he would make his living selling liquor.

Back in Durham, Markham's health began to fail. He left his trackside shanty for the County Home in 1937, paying his own expenses there and reminiscing with the white friends who came to visit. He died on November 11, Armistice Day, 1940. His funeral service was conducted by Father F.W. O'Brien of Immaculate Conception Catholic Church and his casket was borne by Frank Fuller, son of American Tobacco general counsel W.W. Fuller; D.W. Newsom, manager of Durham County; R.B. Nichols, superintendent of the County Home; Percy Reade, county attorney; and lawyer Ludlow Rogers.

He was laid to rest, with the tombstone he had secured well ahead of time, in the gravesite he had bought in the old Fitzgerald family plot, just over the property line from the public cemetery where lay Durham's other leading citizens.

Also ceremoniously laid to rest, 10 years earlier in Maplewood proper, was John Harward, Durham County's sheriff of 23 years. First Baptist pastor Ira Knight and Temple Baptist pastor C.E. Byrd shared ministerial duties, and honorary pallbearers included the county commissioners and state supreme court justice W.J. Brogden while deputies actually carried the load. County offices closed in tribute the afternoon of Harward's funeral. The *Morning Herald* obituary concluded, "His death perhaps brought a more genuine note of sorrow throughout this and adjoining counties than that of any one event that has taken place here in many years."

No doubt. Once county authorities began sorting through the records of Harward's tenure in office, they found his accounts $176,000 short. In those days, North Carolina's county sheriffs still had the duties of tax collector and Harward had been writing off the obligations of friends in the city's business community for years.

The scandal led to reorganization and appointment of Durham County's first manager, Newsom, who needed a decade to get the county's books out of the red. It also gave impetus to the idea, which Kenneth Boyd advocated in the final chapter of his *Story of Durham*, to merge the governments of city and county. In the interest of efficiency and logic, the idea seemed a good one, but good ideas do not necessarily allow for political realities, such as the fact that duplication of government means duplication of patronage opportunities.

With power bases being soundly established in both city hall and county courthouse, notably those of the police and sheriff's departments, and despite widespread support on the part of business interests and regular folks both, proposals for city-county "consolidation," "unification," and "merger"—as it has been termed for various initiatives—have gone down to defeat at the hands of public authorities or the voters in 1933, 1936, 1961, 1974, and 2000. On each occasion, opposition has latched onto details of the particular proposals to make its case—governing council structure, for example—and kept clear power playing couched in euphemism, especially as race became part of the equation.

In the Bull City, though, even euphemism can be colorful. Claude Jones, a leading merger opponent in 1974, characterized the proposed new charter as "some utopian idea" promoted by "someone from Atlanta or Chapel Hill."

African-American political power had been growing in Durham since back in the time of Thomas Hocutt's lawsuit. In 1935, North Carolina Mutual executive C.C. Spaulding convened a meeting that led to the formation of the Durham Committee on Negro Affairs, its name later changed to Durham Committee on the Affairs of Black People. The Committee joined in earlier efforts to register blacks to vote and, by 1939, 68 percent of those eligible were on the Durham County lists. Other pressing concerns south of the railroad were "shanty housing;" parks, pools, and schools for African Americans; and black policemen and better patrolling in Hayti and the other black sections of town. Cheering and prodding the Committee's and others' chipping at Jim Crow's realities, there was Louis Austin and his newspaper the *Carolina Times*, part of a national group of African-American periodicals that kept black news and views visible.

Scandal, segregation, Depression. The textile general strike was the biggest work stoppage in United States history to that point, closing the mills of Durham

LOUIS AUSTIN. This publisher of the Carolina Times *took Durham's African-American elite to task for timidity in the early years of the Civil Rights Movement. (Courtesy of Durham County Public Library.)*

for several weeks in September 1934, idling 7,000 workers, and creating "poor business conditions" both in the factory neighborhoods and downtown. Socialist and former Presbyterian preacher Norman Thomas came to town, lodging at a Hayti hotel, and urged the strikers to "Show your power" in a rally at the ballpark:

> This may be El Toro Park, but I'm not going to throw any bull. The merchants of Durham ought to be on the picket lines. Figures show that 80 percent of all the buying in the country is done by people earning less than $1,000 a year. The only hope of the merchants is for the worker to make more so he can buy more.

As the strike dragged on, Durham's annual fall housecleaning of vice enjoyed an auspicious start with 16 arrests the first morning on charges of vagrancy, soliciting, and immorality, and one of selling high-proof "Injun Oil" to gullible country folk at 25¢ a bottle.

"We don't want any voodoos or conjurers around here," declared Judge James Patton, perhaps concerned by recent happenings at the courthouse. A revolver accidentally went off one day, followed the next by a passing hurricane that broke a substantial limb from an oak tree on the lawn—events that set superstitious eyebrows rising around town.

Not that life in Durham did not have its lighter sides. When John Sprunt Hill feared a run on his Durham Bank and Trust, he restored public confidence by passing cash out the bank's back window to friends who would walk around to the front door, come in, and make deposits. Through hard times, depressed people kept up the trade in liquor, cigarettes, and movies. Durham's industries, licit and otherwise, could supply the first two, while the latter found local street scenes sharing silver screens with Clark Gable and the Wizard of Oz, thanks to traveling cameraman Lee Waters of Lexington, North Carolina. Waters visited Durham three times, twice in 1937 and again in 1940, shot film of people going about the sidewalks and schoolyards, then projected them as selected short subjects before feature films. It made a good living for a photographer forced out of his studio by circumstances of the New Deal age.

During auction seasons, Durham's warehouse district supported a sideshow culture of Bible thumpers, con artists, politicians, ladies of dubious virtue, and street musicians. The Bull City became a mecca for players of the Piedmont Blues, a lively, good-time form of urban folk music quite distinct from its slow and plaintive relation bred in the Texas cane fields and Mississippi Delta. After the warehouses closed, Hayti had liquor houses and parties that wanted dance tunes. Bluesmen could manage a living there, especially if their earnings remained off the records of the county welfare department, and several became well-known recording artists: Reverend Gary Davis, Blind Boy Fuller, Sonny Terry, Willie Trice, and Brownie McGhee.

BLUESMAN SONNY TERRY. Terry was one of the street musicians who played outside Durham's tobacco warehouses during auction seasons in the 1930s. (Jim Sparks photo, courtesy of The Herald-Sun.*)*

Most died broke, their incomes ill-spent or siphoned off by white agents and producers, but their names were remembered and their music preserved by a later generation of white folkies who sought the veterans out during the pop-folk craze of the early 1960s and the Movement-motivated scholarship of the next decade.

Along with the homespun talent, Durham was entertained by star performers from the outside world. One instance produced an unusual twist on the race arrangement. On November 20, 1932, tenor Roland Hayes appeared at the Carolina Theatre. His program included Mozart's "Dans un Bois Solitaire," Schubert's "Nacht und Traume" and "Wohin?", Brahms's "In Waldeseisnsamkeit," and a selection of spirituals. His concert was sponsored by the YWCA and the Brotherhood of St. Joseph's AME Church. Hayes himself was an African American. For the occasion, the Carolina's usual seating pattern was reversed, black patrons getting the orchestra and whites the upper balcony.

Later in the 1930s, Duke undergraduate Les Brown was working up a sideline as a big-band leader. One fellow he entertained with free on-campus shows was a chronically broke law student from California, Dick Nixon. Nixon lived in a shack in the woods a mile from the law school, without electricity or plumbing and, since he was on scholarship, tended his grades with religious zeal. He would take breaks on fall Saturdays to yell himself hoarse at football games, for Duke, having hired coaching master Wallace Wade away from Alabama, had become as famous for football as it was for reading minds.

Duke's Blue Devils were so good that they earned Rose Bowl invitations in 1938—when the "Iron Dukes" went undefeated, untied, and unscored-upon until the last minute of the Pasadena game—and 1941. That second bid would quickly bring to Durham the effect of World War II.

After the Japanese attacked Pearl Harbor, California authorities called off all large public gatherings for fear they would be tempting bomb targets. Facing cancellation of the big game, Duke and Durham issued an invitation of their own to play the game at Duke Stadium. The invitation was accepted and New Year's Day in Durham could only serve to remind any visiting Californians what they were missing, since it brought a taste of typical Carolina January: overcast, cold, and raining. Even so, a Rose Bowl parade rolled down Main Street, spectators overflowed the stadium and temporary stands, and Duke demonstrated its Southern hospitality, losing the game to Oregon State by a score of 20 to 16.

9. WHAT IN THE WORLD?

The city's decline began in 1946.

So said a headline on the *Durham Morning Herald*'s front page of March 23, 1959. The story was the second in a week-long series on the city's faltering economy. Since the end of World War II, Durham had fallen from second to fourth among central North Carolina's five manufacturing centers, from third place to last in wholesale sales, industrial employment had dropped 19 percent since 1947, and its average weekly wage, $64.41, was the lowest among Durham, Raleigh, Greensboro, Winston-Salem, and Charlotte. Sales in the downtown business district had gone down, while those of the other cities went up.

Troubles downtown, particularly the congestion created by its haphazard, unplanned pattern of narrow streets—a "medieval warren," architect George Pyne called it—had dominated a broadcast panel discussion by city leaders during the centennial celebration in 1953. (Creation of the Durham's Station post office was the specific anniversary; the 50th anniversary of the town's incorporation occasioned a semicentennial bash in 1919.) A rush-hour ban on on-street parking was imposed as a relief measure in 1958 but soon backfired. Merchants quickly found the ban made business even worse, so the city council killed it after two weeks.

Downtown parking policies would provide an ongoing comedy for the rest of the twentieth century. In 1981, parking was banned in certain disreputable areas to discourage the drug trade. The next year, a convicted dealer's transfer from the county jail to the state penitentiary was delayed until the city could collect for a parking ticket. In 1986, the levy of increased parking fines was held up because the new tickets arrived with a misprint. The next year, police dealt out tickets on Martin Luther King's birthday, violating the city rule of free parking on holidays.

Kidding aside, the real forces affecting downtown, and the events described as Durham's decline, were more serious than parking and bigger than the business district. The post-war age set off a nationwide desertion of inner cities for suburbia, and a dynamic in Durham's civic life that carries on more than half a century later.

Durham's environs were first to feel the effects of approaching war. In May 1941, news came out that the United States Army, with the active encouragement of chambers of commerce in Roxboro, Oxford, and Durham—particularly Durham chamber secretary Frank Pierson—was considering setting a training camp on 35,000 or so acres of prime tobacco land at the junction of Person, Granville, and Durham Counties. The rolling region of small farms and crossroads communities about 15 miles northeast of the city was along an unprofitable spur of the Seaboard Air Line railroad.

As the summer progressed, so did persuasive efforts of town boosters, such that the camp was, for most practical purposes, a done deal by the time the several hundred families living there could mobilize against it. The opposition had support from the county planning office, but, then as now, reasoned plans were no match for opportunistic visions. Petitions, visits to the War Department in Washington, "Posted" signs, and front-porch stands taken with shotgun in hand all did little good. The camp reservation was reduced to 30,000 acres, thus sparing the Ellis farm of northeastern Durham County, depicted as "Tobaccoland, U.S.A." in a promotional film made by Liggett and Myers.

Four hundred twenty-five families were forced off the land, some of whom had been there for generations, 16 churches closed and disbanded, leaving a residue of bad feeling that was largely overwhelmed by the 35,000 GIs and civilian employees who occupied Camp Butner beginning in June 1942. For Durham, although officials warned against citizens expecting, and so creating, a speculative boom, the camp was a windfall and something of a systemic shock.

A GI FAMILY ARRIVING IN DURHAM. Wives, children, and overloaded cars flooded the city's housing stock as they came to be close to their men at Camp Butner. (Ben Patrick photo, courtesy of the North Carolina Collection at the University of North Carolina.)

STEMMERS AT WORK IN A TOBACCO FACTORY, 1949. During World War II, Durham produced 25 percent of the nation's cigarettes, a commodity so vital to wartime morale that, it is said, Durham was on a list of German bombing targets. (Courtesy of North Carolina Division of Archives and History.)

The Bull City's most popular smoke, Lucky Strike, became the "cigarette that went to war"—switching its packages from green to white in response to military demand for the chromium that went into green ink. Soldiers' wives and children poured into town to be near their men in camp, exhausting the stock of rental housing and creating a market for homeowners' extra rooms. A bus company formed, its entire business the run between Durham and Butner, and the railroad put on special trains from which soldiers tossed candy bars to kids in the backyards passing by. As many as 4,000 GIs might be seen on Durham's streets on any given day, in search of recreation and amusement, and arrests for "immorality" rose proportionately. Four USO clubs opened, three white and one African American, where girls left behind treated boys to touches of home and, in many cases, formed permanent liaisons. One Saturday in the spring of 1943, a "sea of khaki" swept into town and swept up every bottle of legal whiskey by lunchtime.

Such stresses on law, order, infrastructure, and tempers inevitably let to trouble. On April 3, 1943, police needed units of the state guard and Camp Butner military police to control a riot in Hayti. A black soldier, Thomas Allen, allegedly pulled a knife in a Fayetteville Street liquor store when an Alcohol Beverage Control official told him he had more liquor-ration books than the law allowed. Seeing the knife, ABC man T.L. Bailey clubbed Allen with a blackjack and called the cops.

By the time a squad car arrived, a crowd of black soldiers and civilians had gathered and the mood had grown ugly. The police car's tires were slashed, windows smashed, radio antenna broken off, and the just-arrived officer was relieved of his weapon and hit at the knees. Another cop, directing traffic, was hit by a rock; another rock went through the window of a bus, injuring the driver; and a black MP on the scene was hit with a jug. Soon, the situation called for tear gas and reinforcements.

Three weeks after Allen's case was settled with a $100 fine and a year's probation, another racial incident came into a Durham courtroom. Doris Lyon, 16, on her way to school on March 30, had refused a bus driver's request, "You niggers get up and get in the back," because there were no available seats in the back. Doris was fined $5, but public accommodations issues turned deadly serious a year later when bus driver Herman Lee Council shot and killed an African-American soldier who refused to get in his customary place. Council was found not guilty.

Such events led to a biracial ministerial committee to improve "racial cooperation." They also brought the African-American community a gesture it had sought for years, black police. Patrolmen Clyde Cox and Allen Samuel walked their first beat on the evening of July 20 and made their first arrest, nabbing

DURHAM POLICE CHIEF H.E. KING (LEFT) WITH PATROLMAN O.E. JOHNSON, 1945. Black officers were added to the Durham force in response to racial violence that broke out as soldiers came to town for rest and good times. (Courtesy of Durham County Public Library.)

Eugene William Horton, "city-employed Negro," for impersonating an officer when they found him sleeping in a closed movie theater.

There was more to come on the race front.

Durham, like all of America, was a changed place after the war. Returning soldiers brought their GI Bills to Duke University, along with little patience for quaint campus customs, such as freshman hazing. Returning soldiers also brought experience in leadership, innovative thinking, and the can-do ethic, along with little patience for "the way we always did it before."

The new energy expressed itself variously. A children's science museum opened at Northgate Park in 1947, and several cultured groups came together as Allied Arts, later the Durham Arts Council, in 1953. Potential energy turned kinetic with building: student apartments on Erwin Road near the West Campus and Medical School, a new Sears, and a new art-deco bus station on East Main Street. Plus, the American and Liggett and Myers factories were expanded. They alone had supplied the nation with a quarter of its wartime cigarette supply, a product considered so vital to American morale that the German Luftwaffe supposedly listed Durham number 5 among its planned United States bombing targets. The Liggett expansion provided the town with a spectacle of engineering, as the company office was moved from the south side of West Main to the north, costing the company not a moment of productivity as electricity, telephones, and even the bathrooms were kept going all the way across the street. But the influx of energy created a political split, the seminal event in what the newspaper called "decline."

THE LIGGETT AND MYERS CIGARETTE FACTORY. Expansion of the factory after World War II required moving the company office across Main Street. The job was accomplished without missing a minute's productivity, as electricity, phones, and plumbing were kept going throughout the move. (Courtesy of The Herald-Sun *library.)*

R.N. HARRIS (THIRD FROM RIGHT) WITH CITY COUNCIL. Harris was the first African-American city councilman in Durham, elected in 1953, a year before the Brown v. Board *decision set off the Civil Rights Movement. (Courtesy of Durham County Public Library.)*

In the early 1940s, a fresh college graduate named Les Atkins involved himself in civic affairs, leading the Jaycees' campaign that brought Durham the new bus depot. The younger set liked Atkins, the old guard did not. Atkins and his friends recognized that African Americans and organized labor were an untapped source of power, so he brought those interests into a three-way alliance with a war hero, the decorated native son Dan Edwards, as their leading man. Edwards beat old-line businessman Aubrey Wiggins in the mayoral election of 1949, kept the job one term, then left to become an assistant secretary of defense. He was succeeded by E.J. "Mutt" Evans, a Jewish businessman supported by Atkins's crowd, the Committee on Negro Affairs, and the labor unions' Voters for Better Government.

Evans's opponent, lawyer James Patton, complained about "bloc voting," calling it "democracy—Russian style." Evans won. The 1951 election also gave Durham its first women on the city council, Kathrine Everett and Mary Duke Biddle Trent, Ben Duke's granddaughter. R.N. Harris became Durham's first African-American councilman in 1953, a good year before the *Brown* v. *Board of Education* decision touched off the national Civil Rights Movement.

During the 1954 campaign for the board of county commissioners, a political advertisement made a point that has characterized Durham politics ever since: "Whether anyone wants to admit it or not, in almost every election in Durham, the greatest concern is over how the Negroes will vote."

STAR SLUGGER GENE OLIVER SIGNING AUTOGRAPHS FOR YOUNG FANS AT DURHAM ATHLETIC PARK, JULY 15, 1957. African-American fans attempting to integrate the stands on opening day that year were repulsed, although the home team's roster included its first black players. (Courtesy of The Herald-Sun *library.)*

Mutt Evans would remain Durham's mayor for 12 years, but the alliance Atkins had created naturally spawned a conservative counterpart, the Durham United Political Education Council, which embraced the old-timers Atkins had elbowed out. The conservative resurgence was considered good for business, but several years of bitter campaigning and back-room decisions only confirmed Durham's roaring old bare-knuckle image.

Requesting anonymity, a city official told the newspaper, "A friend in Raleigh asked me, 'What in the world is the matter with you folks over there?' "

For the first time in six years, Mayor Evans faced opposition in 1957. That summer, Durham experienced its first sit-in.

With the Brown decision, the Montgomery bus boycott, and a demonstration at the whites-only restaurant at Charlotte's new Douglas Airport, activity was heating up in the budding Civil Rights Movement. Opening day of 1957 saw the Durham Bulls' first three African-American players take the field at Durham Athletic Park and a group of black spectators blocked when they tried to integrate the grandstands. Duke University admitted that three black teachers were coming for a summer program on campus, but quickly explained that the program was government sponsored and the university had to abide by the government's rules. In May, the Durham Interdenominational Ministers Alliance passed a resolution against segregation and called upon Durham's religious institutions to "take the initiative in creating a community free of discrimination."

On June 15, a *Carolina Times* editorial blasted the Durham Committee's leadership for timidity, quoting Thomas Paine: "These are the times that try men's souls," and declaring, "The struggle for human dignity . . . must not be sacrificed on the altar of greed and power merely to obtain a few crumbs for the few."

At this point, the young minister of Asbury Temple Methodist Church, Douglas Moore, had drawn together a group of young activists called "ACT." Sunday afternoons, they met at the church to talk about issues of the day and how to push the envelope of Jim Crow's law. Moore had known Martin Luther King when they were both students at the Boston University School of Theology: Moore thought King was too quiet to make much of a leader on social issues. Since arriving in Durham, Moore had petitioned to integrate the main public library and the city-owned Carolina Theatre and had attempted to swim at a white-only pool at a city park.

Sunday, June 23 was hot and muggy. Later, Moore would rather disingenuously claim the group just wanted to cool off, so they up and went for ice cream. Others who went along though, do agree that what they did that afternoon had not been long in the planning. They left the church and drove up Roxboro Street to Royal Ice Cream. At the corner of Roxboro and Dowd, Royal Ice Cream stood at the

THE REVEREND DOUGLAS MOORE. Moore led Durham's first civil rights sit-in on June 23, 1957 at the Royal Ice Cream Parlor. (Courtesy of Alex Rivera.)

edge of a black neighborhood. However, its entrances and parlors were separated as strictly white and "colored," the colored section so small there was rarely a place to sit. The seven young adults and their minister went in the back, knowing they would be blocked at the white doorway, but instead of waiting to order on their customary side of the shop, they continued through the swinging door into the white parlor, sat down, and waited for what would happen.

They were asked to leave, but they instead asked for ice cream. The situation was more awkward than tense at first, a waiter and then the manager trying to keep things polite. One of the group left. Presently the police arrived, the demonstrators were arrested, and the incident became a test case, the defense appealing one conviction after another until they reached the state supreme court, which upheld the lower courts' finding of trespass. Later that summer, a black tennis player was arrested for using the white courts at Forest Hills Park, although only a few weeks afterward, the courts were open for an all-black tournament.

Two black parents brought suit to have their daughters Elaine Richardson and Joycelyn McKissick admitted to Durham High School. McKissick's father Floyd was an activist attorney and the first black to attend the University of North Carolina law school. He played an increasingly prominent role as the Movement developed, organizing Durham's chapter of the Congress of Racial Equality in 1962 and becoming a close associate of such other civil rights leaders as Ralph Abernathy, James Farmer, and Martin Luther King. Floyd McKissick Jr., who was carrying child-size picket signs before he was 10 years old, remembers that "The thing that would set you apart in that era were things that other people didn't have at their homes, like daily bomb threats." When Movement leaders came to visit and talk tactics, football players from North Carolina College and African Americans who owned guns took sentry duty at the McKissick home. "A lot of it," the younger McKissick says, "you just came to take for granted. It was exciting. It was fun."

Serious fun. Sparked by the Royal Ice Cream incident, protests went on for years. Durham's white schools accepted their first few black students in 1959, including Joycelyn McKissick. Pickets patrolled establishments where African Americans could shop, but not work, and others where they might work, but not eat: Winn Dixie and A&P grocery stores, Kress and Walgreen's, the very fashionable Ellis Stone department store, the downtown Palms Restaurant, and Howard Johnson's on the boulevard to Chapel Hill, where great crowds of demonstrators arrived as soon as churches let out on Sundays.

Black youngsters, high school and college age, carried out the most active protesting, sometimes with the open support of their elders and sometimes in spite of some elders' better judgment. In Durham's well-to-do and privileged African-American circles, there was a degree of content conservatism that kept its distance from confrontation—at least, so far as the eye could see. White Duke students took up the cause, too. Harry Jackson, editor of Duke's alumni publications, wrote a history in 1969 of civil rights activity at the university. At the time, his 80-page report went no farther than his desk and office closet.

A SEGREGATING SIGN AT THE DURHAM BUS STATION. An unidentified man is reminded of his place here at the corner of Chapel Hill and Mangum Streets in the 1940s. The post office is visible in the background. (Courtesy of the Library of Congress.)

Jackson, one of the literary set that formed around English professor William Blackburn and weighed issues of the day at Maola's Chili House and the Ivy Room, related how white students and professors joined the protests downtown in January 1961. Eight months later, Duke matriculated four African-American graduate students, but denied a charter to a campus chapter of the NAACP. Black undergraduates arrived in 1963 in time to hear Alabama Governor George "Schoolhouse Door" Wallace speak in Page Auditorium. In the meantime, the two races were mingling socially in night-spots off campus, such as the Triangle Coffee House and Triangle Professional Theatre on Broad Street. "A great cultural center, as long as it lasted," recalls Jake Phelps, a reporter and activist of that era. Offended neighborhood businesses eventually pressured the cultural center out of existence, but on the far side of town, whites and blacks met and mingled with rhythm and blues at the Stallion Club.

Other things were changing at Duke. A new president, Douglas Knight, fired up by academia's great expectations of the baby boom and federal research grants, set the university on an abortive "Fifth Decade" course of expansion. The school's athletic stature rose with the basketball team's three trips to the national finals, and fell as its formerly powerhouse football program began a decades-long adventure in bathos. The Psychology Department at last shed J.B. Rhine.

Duke was still famous for the ESP laboratory, but the notoriety only embarrassed orthodox scholars and their image-conscious colleagues in administration. Rhine realized that his name and international reputation were all that stood between parapsychology and the campus gate so, in 1962, just before his mandatory retirement, he created the private Foundation for Research on the Nature of Man to carry on his work. The foundation set up headquarters in a large white house that faced Duke's East Campus—the old Trinity—across Buchanan Boulevard and went its independent way under Rhine's direction. Still, Duke's telepathic connection endured in the public mind, invoked on the 1960s television show *Mission Impossible* and *The X-Files* in the 1990s.

Eccentricity was far from done with Buck Duke's college, though. In 1934, Duke hired Dr. Walter Kempner, formerly of the Kaiser Wilhelm Institute for Cellular Physiology and one of the tide of Jewish scholars getting out of harm's way in Europe. Kempner was interested in the effects of diet on disorders such as diabetes and high blood pressure. Finding that those diseases were rare among populations that subsisted heavily on rice, he did some chemical tinkering and came up with a healthy regimen of fruit, juice, vitamins, and rice, keeping protein to a minimum and completely eliminating fat and salt.

His diet was boring at best, and Kempner admitted it, but it seemed to work, especially after two months on the rice regimen in 1942 restored a patient to health from failing kidneys and an enlarged heart. Over the next two years, Kempner successfully treated more than 2,000 more cases, published his results to a skeptical medical establishment, and observed, to his surprise, that his dieters not only improved their kidney and cardiovascular systems, they were also losing weight.

RICE DIET FOUNDER WALTER KEMPNER (CENTER). He partakes here of his own admittedly boring weight-loss regimen at the Rice House on Mangum Street. (Courtesy of Duke University Archives.)

Since the 1890s health fad, Americans had become more and more fixated on the svelte self-image. The post-war product boom brought, with TV dinners, weight-loss concoctions such as Metrecal and Sego. Kempner began treating obesity in the mid-1940s and his business volume grew to the point that, in 1949, the Rice Diet opened its Rice House, a combination boarding house and clinic, off-campus at 1111 North Mangum Street. It was not only plain-folk overeaters who made the Durham pilgrimage. After Betty Hughes, wife of the governor of New Jersey, praised the Rice Diet in the pages of *Ladies Home Journal* in 1968, the Bull City became a mecca for the rich, famous, and fat.

Kentucky Fried Colonel Harlan Sanders and Ben Cartwright from *Bonanza*, a.k.a. actor Lorne Greene, came. Elvis sightings were reported time and again and a rumor spread that the King was living incognito in a railroad caboose parked on a West Durham sidetrack. Frances Bavier, "Aunt Bea," arrived from Mayberry in 1965, joining the ranks that included diet guru-to-be Norman Pritikin, sporting oddsmaker Jimmy "the Greek" Snyder and comedian Buddy Hackett. Hackett came to lose so often, he became a regular Durham personality, even though, once arriving late with a female entourage at the Festa Room restaurant, he was rebuffed by a waitress: "Buddy Hackett, Buddy Schmacket, can't you see we're closed?" (According to Jean Renfro, who wrote a popular book as well as a folklore master's thesis on the Rice Diet, Hackett was permanently banned from the Rice House after pouring salt into a day's worth of urine samples. The imperious Kempner apparently did not get the joke.)

Durham, which in years past had dubbed itself "Chicago of the New South," "The Friendly City of Education and Industry," and "The City of Exciting Stores," found itself declared "Fat City" by no lesser authority than the cover story of the March 1973 *Esquire* magazine, which described not only the Teutonic strictness with which Kempner ruled his customers, but the shenanigans that Ricers pulled to make the discipline and monotony tolerable. Young men of the city were not slow to take advantage of what rapid weight loss did to female dieters' libidos. When a motel that had catered to Ricers was sold in the 1970s, an urban legend holds, the new owners found almost every bed frame had been crushed. Of course, cheating a-plenty of other kinds went on, especially in the "Sin City" strip of doughnut shops, pizza joints, and burgers just across Interstate 85 from the Rice House. For patrons of coffee shops after the bars had closed, a familiar sight was huge Cadillacs riding barely above the pavement as backsliders made the rounds.

Kempner's diet spun off several imitators, and the taking off of flab and taking out of cholesterol became an industry as Durham's economy diversified just in the nick of time.

In 1959, nobody ever thought of such, although someone could and should have. In the roaring old place, some things had never changed. Downtown pool halls and beer joints, frequented by local folk as well as college students who derided them as "grits," but sought from their company a bit of "real life," doubled as well-known bookie parlors. Men of business left their offices to their

COLONEL HARTMAN BUNN, 1948. A spirit of the "roaring old place" has endured in Durham through the years. Here, Bunn creates a sensation—and a Life magazine feature—with a snake-handling convention just a block off Main Street. (Charles Cooper photo, courtesy of The Herald-Sun.)

secretaries while they caught skin-flick matinees at the city-owned, privately leased Criterion Theatre. At the Blue Light drive-in, down in the old Pinhook hollow, carhops would deliver a bucket of chicken along with a cold Blue Ribbon while members of the rowdy set waited to get into a fight.

Legends took root and grew, especially among the high school crowd to which the drug culture trickled down from campus in the 1960s. Duke football player Robin Bodkin won renown in 1967 when he was accosted by 10 armed African Americans and put them to flight single-handedly, a feat taken national in the pages of *Sports Illustrated*. An academic folklore journal recorded another athlete, linebacker Dick Biddle, as being remembered in town—accurately or not, it made a good story—as "the real killer-man, the one who when he left Duke had about 50 civil offenses against him, everything from punching out officers to pissing on funeral homes."

The early post-war years were far from the static and sterile decade supposed by popular present hindsight, to which it seems beyond grasping that *Ozzie and Harriett* and *Father Knows Best* were not documentaries and that middle America enjoyed such televised novelties as no more than the light and fanciful comedies they were meant to be. In 1947 and 1948, the city was enlivened by the spectacles of Colonel Hartman Bunn, who began a snake-handling ministry at his Zion

Tabernacle, just off East Main Street near the downtown Sears store. Durham rated a photo spread in *Life* magazine when Bunn held a convention for takers-up of serpents. For several days in January 1954, Durham joined a national craze with a visitation by flying saucers.

Getting back to business, though, as the *Morning Herald* found, the years from 1947 to 1959 saw genteel decline and a foreshadowing of times to come when no one could, or would, catch on to just what was going on.

In 1959, commerce was being drawn away from the old downtown and to centers that were closer to the people. Durham's first shopping center, Forest Hills, was begun in 1955, followed in the next five years by Wellons Village on the east side and Northgate, just off the Interstate 85 right of way. The downtown Center Theater, whose air conditioning had attracted patrons as much as what was on its screen back in the 1930s, closed after the run of *Dr. Zhivago* in 1966 and reopened at a new center on the site of old Lakewood Park.

With such unsettling developments began the litany of "Do something about downtown," which goes on to this day, and a venerable line of schemes to make it all better. First came the debacle of urban renewal through the 1960s and 1970s, which leveled block after block of admittedly rundown buildings and some not so. One of the city's losses was Southgate Jones Sr.'s home on Chapel Hill Street, its "quiet majesty" replaced by a motel. Before he died in 1949, Jones had wanted to donate the house, its curiosities, and his own collection of tobacco memorabilia to the city, dreaming of their use for a museum of Durham. The city manager never returned his calls.

Renewal, of the 1960s destroy-in-order-to-save style, further surrounded the inner-city warren with a confusing and frustrating one-way Loop that served more as moat than thoroughfare. Plus, the architectural and emotional landmark Union Station was removed in favor of the Loop and a parking garage. Yet another layer of resentment along the city's racial dividing line was laid—re-symbolized by a new freeway that paralleled, in more ways than one, the railroad track.

In 1959, some outcomes of the Civil Rights Movement might have been glimpsed, though it would not be until the following winter that students from North Carolina College would follow their fellows at Greensboro's North Carolina A&T to their local Woolworth's lunch counter and Martin Luther King would arrive for a tour of inspection and a rousing speech at White Rock church. Durham's horizons then, however, like those of most other places, did not extend so far as to reveal such phenomena to come as eco-consciousness and its local spinoff, neighborhood organizing. One other new horizon had been glimpsed, but was, for the most part, about to be lost.

Coming out of World War II, North Carolina was around 47th among the 48 states in per capita income, its economy dependent upon the low-paying manufacture of furniture and fabric and upon agriculture. Responsible citizens—notably Luther Hodges, a retired textile executive who went into politics and found himself in the governor's office upon the death of William Umstead, the only North Carolina chief executive elected from Durham County, in 1954—

looked for ways to improve, making the United States' first gubernatorial expedition to Europe in quest of trans-Atlantic business and preaching economic development and vocational training at home.

Hodges got an earful from Greensboro businessman Romeo Guest, who had been dazzled and inspired by the possibilities of industrial-academic cross-fertilization he saw going on around Boston while he was a student at Massachusetts Institute of Technology. Guest had the brainstorm of capitalizing on the proximity of three research-minded schools near the middle of North Carolina—Duke, the University of North Carolina, and State College in Raleigh—to develop a manufacturing hub he called a "Research Triangle."

Hodges bought the idea. So did Wachovia Bank Chairman Robert Hanes in Winston-Salem, former Wachovia president Archie Davis, New York financier Karl Robbins, and Durham banker George Watts Hill Sr., son of John Sprunt Hill and grandson of George W. Watts. The governor established a Research Triangle Development Council in 1955, headed by sociologist George Simpson, a protégé of University of North Carolina professor Howard Odom, a long-time and much-criticized scholar of Southern society and economics. In 1956, they began pitching the idea to the movers and shakers of Raleigh, Chapel Hill, and Durham.

Not all who heard the pitch caught the enthusiasm of Guest and Hodges. Frank Pierson, by this time executive vice president of the Durham Chamber of Commerce, the man who had labored so hard and well to land the Camp Butner deal 15 years before, was against the idea. Durham's business brotherhood, rolling along with their cigarettes and cotton, figured any benefits from such a pie-in-the-sky notion would just accrue to Raleigh anyway, and maybe Chapel Hill. Their attitude became a self-fulfilling prophecy. While even the village of Morrisville, near the airport and closest municipality to the proposed park, started making plans (never realized) to accommodate an influx of researchers and those who would trade with and upon them, Durham dragged heel for years. There was the water business, which park promoters thought should come from Durham's copious sources and modern system: The city hedged around who was going to pay how much and who would control the tap. There was housing for the executives expected to arrive: Raleigh had a new, northern subdivision, its suburb Cary was almost all white, Chapel Hill was a prestigious address, but when prospective park tenants were given a tour of Durham, they got an eyeful of the slums. One visitor's impression was fixed when he passed a front yard complete with a mule. Even Durham residents were heard to call their "dear, dirty" hometown—as Duke English professor Buford Jones put it, paraphrasing James Joyce on Dublin—the Research Triangle's weak link.

With ready support and participation from other quarters—even western Durham, where Duke president Hollis Edens and chemists Paul Gross and Marcus Hobbs jumped right into the planning—the park took shape over 5,500 acres, all within a section of southeastern Durham County undeservedly known as a "dark corner." The Chemstrand company announced that it was coming in 1959 and, the next year, the federal government said it would add some scientific

GOVERNOR LUTHER HODGES. He looks pained as he helps break ground for an early tenant at the Research Triangle Park. Hodges was one of the driving forces behind the park's creation in the late 1950s. (Courtesy of North Carolina Division of Archives and History.)

agency offices and labs. Durham's first real suburb, Parkwood, took in its first residents as John F. Kennedy's New Frontier was opening.

Some in Durham, such as the *Herald* reporter Russell Clay, realized and publicized the fact that something very big was upon the Bull City's threshold and that it was already past time to get ready with land-use planning, city-county coordination, zoning code updates, and building infrastructure to meet the coming needs. Some others were looking other ways for, in Durham, the 1960s were anything but Camelot. In all fairness, it must be acknowledged that there would be plenty else to keep Durham too distracted to notice that a metropolis was shaping up around it: the surgeon general's report, the flower children, the outside agitators, and what was, from evidence and experience, a very real possibility of all that was familiar going up in smoke, not of the tobacco persuasion.

A recognition of mutual interest and a pattern of cooperation across race and class lines that appeared after World War II was replaced by a reversion to and hardening of antagonism and distrust as the Civil Rights Movement careened past integration under law toward what looked like anarchy and opportunism. One illustrative and long-remembered incident was that of the Malcolm X Liberation University.

After African-American students occupied Duke's administration building on February 13, 1969, and as Durham reeled from another round of curfews after a downtown demonstration degenerated into looting and window-breaking down Main Street, community organizer Howard Fuller—an individual most members of the white power structure blamed for Durham's worsening race relations, while others gave him credit for keeping them from explosion—opened an alternative college in an old warehouse. The announced idea was to educate blacks in their history and in self-help skills they could use to develop businesses of their own.

From that seemingly reasonable point, though, Fuller went on to demand money for his project: in particular from white religious groups. Some actually obliged, including a good-works fund of the national Episcopal Church, which chipped in $45,000. Individual Episcopalians expressed their feelings where they would have the greatest effect, in the churches' collection plates, creating financial crises for their parishes and the diocese of North Carolina that was only made worse when the home office in New York refused to reveal how or why it had decided to hand Fuller the money. Still worse was that Malcolm X Liberation University, after moving to Greensboro in 1970, slipped out of business and existence with never an accounting. Fuller himself returned to his native Milwaukee.

On the other hand, while bulldozers and rebuilders were having their way uptown, the reincarnation of Hayti, assumed and expected by the African-American interests that had signed onto the idea of urban renewal in the first place, never happened. Like Malcolm X Liberation University, the promise of new investment bringing new opportunity and wealth to the region below the railroad, as well as to the city center in general, disappeared, taking hopes, expectations, and money and leaving a litany of "promises unmet" to be repeated for years and years ahead.

10. Born Again, Bicentennially

There were chickens, there were cows and sheep and hogs, there was barbecue and a moonshine still. There were clog-dancers and weavers and an old guy with a Gabby Hayes beard selling silver jewelry. There was a peg-legged medicine-show pitchman, clumping along the flagstone walks with a Budweiser in his hip pocket. There was gospel music, for heaven's sake. And it was all out in the open, in plain sight of a wedding party gathered for photos before the Duke Chapel, a Gothic cathedral in miniature where piney woods had ruled 50 years before, and of the brazen stare of Buck Duke's statue, not to mention in easy flick of his cigar.

It was 1974 and the Bull City was about to go country.

The occasion was a post–flower power renewal of Duke University's Joe College Weekend rite of spring, taking the form of a festival of North Carolina folklife, brainchild of Texan undergraduate George Holt. Little could anyone have suspected that vernal evening, but in the next few years, the festival and its creator would be taken off campus to lead Durham into rediscovering and redefining itself.

By 1974, Durham was a mess. A massive effort at slum clearance and rebuilding had been discussed since 1940 and undertaken in the early 1950s, producing the city's first public-housing projects: Few Gardens, in the East Durham mill-village area, for whites, and McDougald Terrace, in a bottom across the Fayetteville Street ridge from Hayti, for African Americans. As the fashion for urban renewal swept the 1950s, the notion of new construction rising where city blight had been, and corollary social engineering, with United States government money paving most of the way, was too good to resist.

An expressway to carry traffic past downtown and relieve the rush hour congestion supposed to be throttling business, downtown and its surroundings cleared off and built over, a new government complex as centerpiece and totem at the heart of Durham, added up to a vision boosted with New Frontier vigor by all the city's brokers of power, not least the Durham Committee on Negro Affairs.

By 1974, all that had been created was a wealth of vacant lots and bad will, and the processes urban renewal was supposed to reverse had only been accelerated. What was overlooked in the can-do frame of mind, and in the period's true belief in progress, was the human element. Slums may have been ratty, but people came up with their own social infrastructures and informal institutions to survive in them. Bulldozers and bright ideas obliterated those along with the shacks and alleys, leaving nothing of value in their place.

South of the railroad, the experience widened the class divide between people in the projects, the remaining slums, and the African-American upper crust of North Carolina College, now North Carolina Central University, and the business community, which could look down from its aerie in the North Carolina Mutual tower, risen on Chapel Hill Street from the old Ben Duke Four Acres estate. Interviewed by the University of North Carolina's Southern Oral History Project in 1999, Lawrence Ridgle of Fay Street in eastern Durham recalled how North Carolina Mutual had foreclosed on his father's Fayetteville Street home when tuberculosis left him unable to keep up mortgage payments, along with other grievances on the part of the firm's working-class customers:

> They had all kinds of little fine clauses in there people couldn't read and they wouldn't pay off claims. And people were afraid, especially—most people were ignorant. My daddy swears that they sold that house that he was buying for them to pay off that first bill . . . first big insurance policy.

Ridgle said his father "used to rub shoulders" with some of "the pillars—those were the millionaires when I was a kid here." Some were civic-minded, not all, particularly one fellow named McDougald:

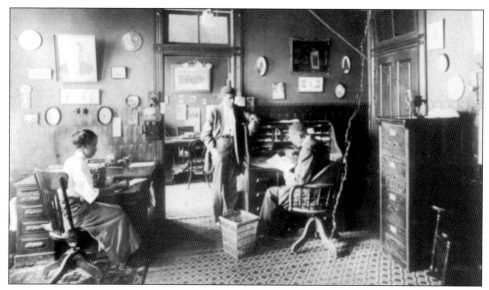

OFFICE OF THE NORTH CAROLINA MUTUAL LIFE INSURANCE COMPANY. This business, established in 1898, was led by black businessmen John Merrick, Aaron Moore, and C.C. Spaulding. (Courtesy of the North Carolina Collection at the University of North Carolina.)

142

McDougald had a lot of tenement houses over there in what they called the Hayti section. Little, run-down—worse than these shacks. When he died, the black people had a parade. They were glad he was dead.

They sold us out. They didn't help the masses. Then they started helping themselves. And I think they stopped black growth. I don't think the white man stopped black growth in Durham. I think what we call our founding fathers, Ed Mert [possibly a transcription error; the context implies Ridgle meant Ed Merrick, son of the N.C. Mutual founder John Merrick], McDougald and Moore. They were the beginning. And the offsprings of that crippled the black, not the whites. Had these raggedy ass tenement houses that they collect rent off of for 50 years. Didn't do anything to them. They were substandard. I know some horses that lived in much better places than blacks did.

Whatever the realities had been, as time went along and renewal did not, Hayti became a myth, a golden-age realm of African-American enterprise, dignity, and self-sufficiency ruined and stolen by white people and their expressway (which actually runs south of where the Hayti business section stood). The image that endures and informs twenty-first century opinions is of the vibrant little Harlem suggested by the 1948 film *Negro Durham Marches On*, a promotion sponsored by the Durham Business and Professional Chain, a black chamber of commerce, while leaving any unpleasant history unspoken of in polite society.

Old Hayti would have died no matter what anyone did to it, for the same reasons as the primarily white business district north of the tracks: people were moving outward and business followed. By the mid-1960s, Durham's African Americans were moving south. The address of choice for the upwardly mobile was among new apartments and houses south of North Carolina Central University, around Fayetteville and Pilot Streets and the present College Plaza Shopping Center. The mom 'n' pop shops and services that characterized Hayti and downtown would not have been able to compete with the retail chains and amalgamations already taking shape.

Making things even worse in the old "medieval warren," clearing and building dragged on for years. For anyone who wanted to buy a tennis racquet at Durham Sporting Goods, see an art film at the Rialto or soft pornography at the Criterion, enjoy an Amos 'n' Andy's hot dog in its natural habitat with upturned Coca-Cola crates for seats, getting there was less and less worth the trouble.

By the time the Loop was done and the new city hall, by the time downtown was declared an official historic district, there were relatively few people around to notice or care. The habit of going downtown was broken, business had jumped the sinking ship and the refrain "I *never* go downtown" was becoming virtually a Bull City motto.

By 1974, "downtown" had long since ceased to be synonymous with "Durham." Powers in other principalities, in other so-called "paradigms," of the city were slouching toward an unforeseeable—if not unimaginable—convergence.

One Saturday morning in 1972, Max Rogers awoke in his Trinity Park home to the song of buzzsaws. Looking out, he discovered a crew hard at work taking down the willow oaks that had grown stately over 50 years of shading the neighborhood. Rogers discovered that the city authorities were planning to drive a thoroughfare his way, linking the central part of town with the broad Hillsborough Road. This being 1972, when the public's business was still usually carried out in private homes on Sundays after church, this was news to Rogers and those around him.

"This was big government at its worst," recalls Eugene Brown, a realtor who lives in the Trinity Park home built by John Spencer Bassett following the Trinity trustees' vote of confidence and a prominent member of the Durham Voters Alliance, one of the two white-and-black political organizations formed in the early 1970s by alumni of the 1960s.

Trinity Park residents got the city enjoined from more tree-trimming, and terminated the thoroughfare project after a massive turnout before the city council, despite one councilman's lament that Durham must not be kept "a sleepy little college town." From that experience developed a neighborhood association, which inspired imitators all over the city, leading to the formation, in 1985, of an Inter-Neighborhood Council that would add its presence and heft to Durham's diversifying political cast.

Around this same time, in fashionable Forest Hills—a 1920s neighborhood at what was then the southern edge of town, Durham's first to be built around a golf course—Margaret Haywood got her dander up when an out-of-town friend told her that a Southern business magazine had referred to Durham as "a hot-dog town," lacking pedigree, taste, and culture.

The friend, Arnold McKeithan, was an attorney for the Norfolk Southern Railroad, which was taking a restored 1830s locomotive, the *Best Friend of Charleston*, on promotional tours. Haywood, history conscious, suggested he bring the engine to Durham on April 26, the anniversary date of both the post office and the Bennett Place surrender. In February 1974, Haywood's husband, Egbert, got a surprise call from McKeithan, saying, "I want to know where to put Mrs. Haywood's train."

With a date set for April 26, 1975, Margaret Haywood figured she needed a committee to promote the *Best Friend*'s appearance. Meanwhile, well aware of the Old Southern plantations that had once graced the northern part of Durham County, she had pulled some lady friends together as "The Pride Builders" with the mission to dispel any more "hot dog" misconceptions. Notice of Haywood's efforts was relegated to the local society pages, but by October 1974, they had piqued enough interest in a variety of circles that the Historic Preservation Society of Durham could become official and hold a meeting. Some historical artifacts went on display for the occasion, including a Bible, pen, and pair of spectacles that had belonged to Bartlett Durham, as well as his license to practice medicine.

Opportunity for more than talk and get-togethers was at hand. In 1973, with the state taking stock of North Carolina's own relics and remains, the 1787

144

THE BARN AT STAGVILLE. Built to last in 1860, this great barn became part of a state historic property thanks to efforts of the fledgling Historic Preservation Society of Durham.

Bennehan House at Stagville went onto the National Register of Historic Places. The property by then was owned by Liggett and Myers. The land was farmed, but the house, for years a tenant residence, was empty except for wasps, and dilapidated, with its approaches grown up in weeds and honeysuckle. Haywood and others from the Preservation Society called on Liggett and Myers president Ray Mulligan and, within a year of the group's founding, secured a promise of the house and 79 acres. For its birthday, the society threw a party for the public at Stagville and 500 members of the public showed up for lemonade, hayrides, singers, dancers, a spinning-wheel demonstration, and a play, *A Day at Stagville 1799.*

Besides its obvious importance for those involved at the time, the Preservation Society's formation and its getting down to brass tacks—or clapboard and pegs, as the case was—meant more in a bigger picture, though that would only become apparent with hindsight. With a handful of exceptions to prove the rule, such as Bennett Place patron R.O. Everett and museum-minded Southgate Jones Sr., historical consciousness was a novelty in Durham.

The "hot-dog" adjective had a point, stated another way in the councilman's 1972 remark about the city's need to cut and pave its way from being "a sleepy little college town." Since World War II, the mood of the age had favored bigger and newer. The past was "old fashioned" and progress was the most important product. Attitudes only advanced the out-with-the-old spirit that was fundamental in the Republic's beginnings. It must have seemed just recognition of the obvious as technology transformed everything, not the least thinking, faster and faster, for the next 200 years.

"ART" IN DURHAM. Two New Yorkers wrote on a sidewalk, broke it up, dumped it in a gully, and went home with $10,000 in commission from a 1989 "public art" conference in Durham. (Kevin Keister photo, courtesy of The Herald-Sun.)

"Renewal" had obliterated the train station and the Jones mansion: Ben Duke's estate, regarded by the university as too much trouble to modernize with air conditioning and such, went down where a modernistic office tower went up, the Durham Hotel—formerly the Jack Tar and before that the Washington Duke— city's pride of 1925, was going to be next, and the Carolina Theatre, the last movie house downtown with its lease running out, appeared ripe to follow. Even in those go-go days, a vanishing landscape unsettled the natives. A feeling was catching that something was going quite wrong.

That wasn't all.

Jim McIntyre, Duke Class of 1971 and a protégé of formidable university culture maven Ella Fountain Pratt, became Allied Arts of Durham's first executive director upon his graduation. Living in an apartment, use of which was part of his pay, and working from a cozy, cramped house on Proctor Street between the old suburbs of Morehead Hills and Forest Hills, McIntyre had taken to heart a notion that arts were, as he told the *Duke Alumni Register,* "not just valuable, but essential" to the community's well-being.

McIntyre was convinced that art came with a spiritual dimension, offering uplift to individuals in an age of alienation. Moreover, where his organization had kept a place among Durham's white elite, McIntyre said, "Allied Arts has to go out into the community and work." The idea was radical to McIntyre's employers, but he was a good salesman.

"Once I had sold myself on community arts," he said in March 1972, "when I once found myself finding satisfaction in the job, I became effective in convincing other people of the value of the arts to Durham, in exciting them about it."

At that point, McIntyre was planning a city-wide festival. Two years later, in September 1974, just a month before the Preservation Society's first meeting, McIntyre took his cause downtown with a Saturday festival that put clog-dancing, sidewalk-drawing, and even country music in full and open public view along Chapel Hill Street.

In a juxtaposition of incongruous elements, the Street Arts Festival stage was set up next to the Republican Party office—itself a symbol of the city's political diversification. Some things had not changed, though. In November 1974, a referendum on city-county merger went down to yet another defeat.

Street Arts, however, became an annual event after a few editions growing to fill a weekend, and half the space within the Downtown Loop. Arts now linked with the still-anticipated reinvigoration of downtown, McIntyre the marketer changed the organization's name to Durham Arts Council and, after the city occupied its new offices in 1977, moved the arts into the old Greek revival city hall, originally built in 1904 for the Central High School. From its place on the fringe, the Arts Council thus made itself a visible and interested player in Durham's economic picture, as well as its aesthetic one.

An alumnus of campus activism, McIntyre, still in his twenties, found affirmation in moving mainstream. "I've discovered you *can* get things done," he said. "You *can* make things happen."

He wasn't the only one.

For decades, Durham's outdoorsy set had used the hills and river valleys north of town for getting back to nature. An Explorers' Club formed at Duke in the 1920s, counting among its members J.B. Rhine who, upon request, conducted sylvan experiments in hypnotism; law school dean Justin Miller, who in the 1930s led a feasibility study on city-county merger; folklorist Frank C. Brown; and the group's founder, Duke Press director Ernest Seeman, who would years later publish his novel of early Durham, *American Gold*.

In 1971, Seeman set down some memories of those hiking exploits, including one encounter with a north-county landowner: "We all advanced toward the grizzled apparition that stood there with a long bushy beard and a lantern, its eyes glowing with rancor and arousement like fire-coals." Spotting campfire smoke, the grizzled apparition had come to investigate and stumbled upon one of Rhine's attempted hypnoses. "Suddenly he exploded with: 'Waal what's thet feller doin' to that woman?' To his provincial and unscientific mind the psychological demonstration going on was plainly nothing less than a devilish rite of witchcraft."

The Eno River had served as the water source for Durham's first municipal system from 1887 to 1927. In the 1920s, the city switched to the Flat River, building a dam and reservoir named Lake Michie, due in part to a public perception of a "filthy Eno," carrying waste from a Hillsborough dye works. By the early 1960s, though, city planners and engineers, recognizing that the

Research Triangle and universities' growth was going to bring a dramatic rise in residential and industrial consumption, looked at the Eno again.

With the idea of "Lake Eno" floated, developers saw the promise of shoreline properties. The city followed, backing an Eno Loop highway, carrying through traffic around Durham and opening the river and reservoir for recreation-challenged residents. What sounded progressive in some quarters sounded an alarm in others, among them river-valley landowners and the nature-loving crowd, in particular one Duke faculty wife.

Margaret Nygard, India-born to English parents, lived with her husband Holger, a folklorist, on a bluff above the river off Cole Mill Road. As formidable a grandmother figure as ever took on a city council, Nygard became the founder and focal point of an Association for the Preservation of the Eno River Valley in 1965.

Nygard and her fellow travelers, such as George Pyne—an architect by trade, naturalist and historian by avocation—went about selling the public on the river's value as it was. A weekend hike series drew 200 the first time out, 450 the second. At the same time, association members investigated the reservoir proposals and found them, at least from their point of view, wanting. They then came up with what they thought were better ideas.

Dismissing the Eno bunch as naysayers and romantics, if not pot smokers with nihilistic tendencies, the downtown powers went about buying up Eno land, paying lip service to a park while still thinking reservoir. Nygard was persistent, though: soft-spoken, and carrying a Valkyrean stature, capturing press attention and eventually favor with her advocacy for a state park to preserve what was, after all, a relatively pristine stream in what was about to become a citified setting.

A final confrontation came in 1970 when preservationists faced off against the bulldozers of a Charlotte developer at West Point. The city adopted the idea of turning its bought land into a park and the Eno Association and its spinoff group, Friends of West Point, found allies in the Daughters of the American Revolution, United Daughters of the Confederacy, and the Junior League as they went about creating a natural-historical reserve.

The old Christian's Mill, which had stood beside the river at the Roxboro road ford since the 1770s, had gone out of business in 1947 and fell victim to a flood in February 1973. However, a paper company in Virginia had an almost identical mill to spare: The preservation-conservation coalition moved the mill down, restored it, and had it ready to run again just in time. In time, that is, for the bicentennial.

Following hard upon the 1960s, upon the grudges and embarrassments left by the Civil Rights Movement, Vietnam, flower power, and Watergate, and with the whole ethos of newer-bigger-better called into question along with everything establishmentarian, the approaching 200th anniversary of American independence brought a wave of social and historical review and reassessment. Small-town festivals and outdoor dramas popped up across the country as a shook-up population found something to celebrate, after all, in their long-neglected past.

MARGARET NYGARD. She led the 1960s campaign to preserve the Eno River from flooding and development, one of several grassroots efforts that combined to dramatically change Durham's personality and self-image. (Harold Moore photo, courtesy of The Herald-Sun.)

George Holt was still in Durham. Bob Chapman, another Duke graduate, had been brought back to town to organize a bicentennial observance. Having seen the success of Holt's two campus folk festivals, Chapman approached Holt about something bigger. Maybe something to open the new park out on the Eno River.

Holt took his festival idea from the Smithsonian Institution's annual Festival of American Folklife in Washington. He went at organizing a Bicentennial Festival of North Carolina Folklife with Smithsonian-like production values, tapping such connections as Smithsonian folklorist Ralph Rinzler, who had discovered such talented North Carolina old-timers as Doc Watson and 1930s Durham bluesmen Sonny Terry and Brownie McGhee; and Alan Jabbour, a former student of Holger Nygard's who had gone to work for the Library of Congress. Helping hands also came from the state Bicentennial Commission; from Liggett and Myers, which sent a blank purchase order to the J.A. Jones Construction Company; and from Duke, which dispatched its landscaping crew to get West Point ready for company by the Fourth of July.

Over its three-day weekend run (July 4, 1976 fell on a Sunday), the festival drew 100,000 people. It was the biggest bicentennial event in North Carolina, even spinning off an "alternative"—in those days of "alternative lifestyles"— "Forklift Festival," an after-hours bash for performers and helpers at the Eno held at an 1850s plantation home turned hippie pad just up Roxboro road.

For many Durham natives, the festival was a revelation. Bluesmen and even a Greek band showed off aspects of the community that had been all but invisible to the city at large. Holt is quoted in a 1978 interview with *Tar Heel* magazine: "The festival ties into Durham in a very big way. And it's something that brings together different parts of the community to work for something larger. And within the unified communities, we're saying, differences are good. We're celebrating diversity."

Twenty years later, "celebrating diversity" would have become a cliche in Durham, often spoken with sarcasm. Still, the folklife festivals went on every Independence Day, taken over by the Eno River Association in 1979 as a money-raising event for state park land along the river. Still marketing-savvy, the Arts Council changed the name of its festival to Centerfest in the 1980s, playing on the campaign for a new civic center downtown. Almost 200 neighborhoods had organized themselves in some form or another. By its silver anniversary, the Preservation Society could count a dozen or more significant saves, with more than 50 Durham County locations added since 1974 to the National Register, including the entire downtown business district, where flamboyant architecture still gave off a sense of bullishness.

Even the Bulls came back. After a 9-year hiatus, including two seasons under the name "Triangles," pro baseball returned to Durham Athletic Park with the Class A, Carolina League Durham Bulls. They would quickly be setting attendance records for the minor leagues and make the town the set and setting for the 1988 hit movie *Bull Durham*, produced by 1966 Durham High graduate Thom Mount.

George Holt went on to become founding director of a folklife office in the state's Department of Cultural Resources, producing a second statewide festival at West Point and a festival of British-American relations for the 400th anniversary of Sir Walter Raleigh's attempted colonies, in 1984. Bob Chapman went on to coordinate the Durham County Centennial in 1981, then took up real estate and the cause of traditional community-New Urbanist design. Margaret Nygard remained in charge of the Eno until her death in 1995. Jim McIntyre left Durham in 1982 to raise money for Carnegie Hall. He subsequently left there to join a circus in New York and lived there until his death in 1998. Trinity Park became one of Durham's most respectable, and still leftish, places to live.

The chamber of commerce, whose previous commissions such as the Kenneth Boyd history of 1925, had extolled industrial growth and men of business who made themselves rich, commissioned another promotion, a movie, in 1983. Its title is *Durham: We Want to Share It With You*. Its opening scene is of a bluegrass band playing by the river at West Point Park.

EPILOGUE: THE WAY THINGS HAPPEN

Well, it didn't all work out that way. The forces and trends working upon Durham through the 1970s and into the 1980s were not all redemptive.

The textile industry, updating its processes and looking overseas, deserted Durham in the early 1970s. Changing shifts at the cigarette factories still created miniature rush hours—lasting maybe 30 minutes—at bicentennial time, but even tobacco was on the way out.

Durham's signature brands, Chesterfield and Lucky Strike, had been steadily losing market share since R.J. Reynolds introduced its filtered Winstons in 1950. Release of the surgeon general's report, definitively linking cigarettes with cancer, in 1964, was met with shrugs and denial, but Durham's plants were getting old and antiquated. American Tobacco's Pettigrew Street complex, including the 1874 Bull Durham factory, closed in the summer of 1987. American moved its operations to Reidsville, about 45 miles northwest. In the later wave of corporate mergers, the company that went by the name of Buck Duke's sprawling trust ceased to exist.

In November that year, Durham sold its last leaf. The tobacco market, never large by comparison with those in the east such as Wilson and Goldsboro, shrank from 13 floors to 1 as companies changed buying practices and weeded smaller markets out. Farmers were already abandoning Durham, its urban-renewed street system rendering the old Tobacco Row more trouble to get to than it was worth, and Durham's last warehouse, Planter's, was located not on once-thronged Rigsbee Avenue but out on Geer Street at the edge of a decaying neighborhood and a seedy industrial district. The only auctioneer's chant Durham would hear would come from a mock sale at the Duke Homestead State Historic Site, held annually for old times' sake.

Liggett and Myers, smallest of the United States' major cigarette producers and floundering for want of a product the public would buy, moved out to Mebane in Alamance County in the summer of 2000, stubbing out the century.

Even as arts moved downtown, businesses moved out. Big stores such as Sears, Belk's, and Thalhimer's were gone to the 'burbs before the second Street Arts Festival. Northgate Mall enlarged in 1972, responding to plans for a rival, South Square, on the Chapel Hill side of town, just across the divide between bypass and business routes of U.S. 15–501 from a fragrant sewage plant. South Square not only drew department stores, but spawned a surrounding community of strip centers, office buildings, and apartments that attracted service, legal, and financial firms out of the city center and into what became, for most practical purposes, a new downtown. Even the Durham Herald Company, whose *Morning Herald* and *Sun* newspapers cheered every new hope for a downtown comeback, found the medieval warren could not accommodate modern times. Its new plant opened in 1990 in the South Square business district. Employees at last had places to park.

A generation later, South Square in turn would shut down almost overnight when a bigger, newer shopping center opened farther south, close to the Research Triangle Park and in the heart of a developmental explosion along Interstate 40 and N.C. 54.

At the time of the county centennial, it appeared that downtown might actually be ready for a comeback. There were the new city hall, new judicial building, and new public library. With dust barely settled from implosion of the Durham Hotel on December 14, 1975, boosters began talking up a new hotel and civic center to bring back downtown. The Arts Council came along with a complementary proposition for renovating its building and the adjacent Carolina Theatre, now an art-movie house run by the nonprofit Carolina Cinema Corporation, into a downtown arts complex. In 1986, private developer Franklin Wittenberg, who

WAREHOUSE OWNER DURWOOD THOMAS, 1987. Thomas inspects leaf at Planter's Warehouse, which was the last of what were once as many as 13 sales floors in Durham. Durham's tobacco market's final season was in 1987. (Harold Moore photo, courtesy of The Herald-Sun.*)*

came to Durham for the Rice Diet, went to work on an office tower for some vacant lots near the old warehouse district.

With fits, starts, cost overruns, delays, embarrassments, and straining patience, all those projects came into being. Yet, downtown remained a realm of vacant storefronts and plywood-faced windows. Business did go on in upper rooms, and some people even took up residence, but to all appearances, inner Durham remained just another deserted and desolated American downtown. A regional orchestra refused to hold rehearsals there, its members fearing for their safety, a concern encouraged by the lowland ring of decaying, drug-ridden slums enclosing the downtown ridge. Even patrons of the library, the theater, and the Bulls made quick their entrances and their exits. As the years went along, proposals for fixing the situation came more and more to resemble what had been there before the Loop.

Those who wished to build, rebuild, and revive Durham—and not only downtown—had to contend not only with competition from other communities nearby, but those communities' invoking Durham's venerable, bare-knuckle, blue-collar, "roaring old" image and making sure it remained in force. Durham hardly helped its own cause by ignoring its problems with crime, housing, and race. Race relations never came back—if, indeed, there was any coming back to do—after the 1960s: they only polarized more over bad memories, distrust, and vicious rhetoric that might be whispered around a neighborhood or flung out in the open at a public meeting.

No issue hits more viscerally than those surrounding schools. While merger of the city and county governments failed again and again, the archaic and racially separative lines between city and county school systems was breached in 1991, mostly by the brute force of county commissioners chairman Bill Bell, first beneficiary of the Durham Voters Alliance clout back in 1972 when, as a young computer engineer, he was elected to the county board. The subsequent school districting and pupil assignment were lightning rods for frustration, anger, fear, and long-held grudges that carried hearings well past the point of civility. Watching a televised meeting, one middle school girl wondered aloud, "Why are those people behaving like that? Don't they know there are children watching?"

Race was not the only dividing line. From the two-way split of the 1950s, city politics evolved into a fluid system of political action groups: the old Durham Committee, the newer Voters Alliance and Peoples Alliance, and the later-forming organization of older-line interests, the Friends of Durham. From the point of view of Durham natives and old-timers, the Alliances, made up of former student activists and members of the preservationist-conservationist-populistic set, many of them recent arrivals to town, were turning their home place out from under them. In 1988, a city council candidate summed up the election's meaning: "It's us against them!"

Of course, the identities of "us" and "them" depended on who was doing the labeling. People Durham born and bred had no less proprietary interest in the city than those others, who were not in all cases outsiders, anyway. The product of this was a paralytic tension that saw the political cast of Durham's nominal leadership flip and flop, right to left to right and back again, every election or two. For those who could not enjoy the comedy, cynicism became conventional wisdom.

As time went by, growth within and around Durham outstripped all projections. From its namesake municipal trio, the Research Triangle area spread with the widening highways and an influx from foreign parts where extended commutes and traffic jams were just the way things were supposed to be. Development north of Durham was held back by the Triassic Basin, where the earth could absorb only so many septic tanks, and by the difficulty of access to the park and airport. Development at Durham's south was just the opposite, turning what had been woodland and tobacco fields as recently as the 1970s into ever-increasing condo clusters, subdivisions, and shopping centers indistinguishable one from another and blurring what was Durham into what were Chapel Hill, Morrisville, and Cary—all those, collectively, as faceless, generic, and disposable as every other airport suburb in the developed world.

Indeed, as the twenty-first century began, it was a good question whether Durham or any of the Triangle's historic towns would long retain any practical identities other than names on a map, or if they would vanish into megalopolitan anonymity as had such south-county crossroads as Lowe's Grove, Brassfield, or Bethesda.

Whatever the fate of its character at the turn of century, Durham lost some of its characters.

Sam Reed, a labor organizer of Depression vintage who had marched in Alabama with Martin Luther King, a Russian immigrant who lost a brother in Red Army service during the Russian Civil War, was a regular before council and commissioners, always calling for keeping King's legacy alive. He was familiar at editorial offices, dropping off copies of his *Trumpet of Conscience* newsletter. He was a charming old Quixote, passionate and colorful no matter what opinions might be held by whomever he happened to collar.

"I'm not anything special," he said. "I'm just an ordinary Joe."

Upon immigrating, Reed had swapped his Russian last name for an American one, that of John Reed, the journalist of Bolshevik sympathies who is entombed at the Kremlin. He saw himself American, one with the country's revolutionary pedigree and, after doing his Army duty in the Second World War by way of Camp Butner, he and his wife Georgia found they had been touched by something in the Bull City. They came back when it was time to retire. "We thought it was a paradise," he said. "There was grass, and trees, and communities." Reed died, well into his 90s, in August 1999.

Oscar Matthews was Durham's town crier. Shellshocked in the Pacific during World War II, he found himself unable to work, but in 1946, he heard the call to preach and spent his days striding downtown streets, stores, and the lobbies of banks, crying "There's a hell on this earth, ain't that right!" or "God knows what's going on, because God knows his business!" or "The devil made you do it, and he's going to get you for it!"

RUSSIAN IMMIGRANT SAM REED WITH HIS WIFE GEORGIA AT HOME. For years, the former labor organizer was a familiar figure at public meetings and newspaper offices, reminding one and all that the old "left" endured. He passed away in 1999. (Jim Sparks photo, courtesy of The Herald-Sun.*)*

Don Schlitz, a Nashville songwriter who grew up in Durham, wrote a tune about him, "Oscar the Angel." Randy Travis put it on an album.

However much he might frighten uninitiates, Oscar was a well-mannered soul. He would quiet down if he passed a church while services were going on. Bumming a quarter, Oscar was told by the prospective bumee that he was out of change, whereupon Oscar handed the fellow a quarter of his own and went about his way. He was dubbed the "Mayor of Main Street" and, for his 67th birthday in 1988, a downtown crowd threw him a party at Wilma's Southern Kitchen across from the Empire State–like Central Carolina Bank building.

"He's like a child, a 2-year-old child with the most beautiful smile I've seen in my life," restaurant owner Wilma Ritchie told a *Morning Herald* writer. "You can feel terrible when you come to work, but he comes in and smiles and it makes you feel good."

For 55 years, Oscar Matthews preached the Lord and made working people happier than they would have been without him. But downtown is a quieter place now: Oscar died November 8, 2001.

Still, as we have seen, in the Bull City some things do not change and some traditions endure.

After Erwin Mills closed up, the West Durham area it had spawned reinvented itself. The miniature business section that faced the mill across Ninth Street became a college-town main street of bookshops, nightspots, boutiques, and everything trendy. Situated between Duke's East Campus and a graduate-student ghetto in the mill houses, Ninth Street drew customers from near and far, intrigued by fresh bagels, socialist newspapers, gelato, running shoes, and the lemonade at Durham's last surviving soda fountain.

And by Fiddlin' Dave McKnight.

In former lives, McKnight was the Duke Blue Devil mascot; a writer of editorials for the *Fayetteville Observer*; a skillful, if stylistically unorthodox, amateur tennis player; a classical violist; a sports fanatic who drove nonstop across country to watch Duke beat Stanford in football in 1971; and a candidate for the Democratic nomination for the United States Senate—he finished fifth in a field of eight in the 1978 primary after a campaign by foot through every one of North Carolina's 100 counties.

In 1974, McKnight and his viola turned up at a Friday-night picking session on what was then-rural Horton Road. Diving into the sound and spirit, he was shortly ripping out "Orange Blossom Special" and "Bragtown Blues," and that fall became one-quarter of the Joel Haswell Revue, closing act for the first Street Arts Festival.

After politics, music became his calling. It took him to Nashville and to Texas, and finally back to Bull City where, lunchtimes and evenings, you'll find him doing his own, personal version of an Oscar role on Ninth Street, usually somewhere near the Regulator Bookshop, established in 1972 by Tom Campbell, once a leftist *Duke Chronicle* editor and a future Durham city councilman.

In Durham, that's the way things happen.

No bull.

FIDDLER DAVID MCKNIGHT, SEPTEMBER 1974. McKnight, of the Joel Haswell Revue, entertained at the Durham Arts Council's first Street Arts Festival. Nowadays, he may be found playing his music on trendy Ninth Street.

BIBLIOGRAPHY

Anderson, Jean Bradley. *Durham County*. Durham: Duke University Press, 1990.

Asbury, Francis. *Francis Asbury in North Carolina: The North Carolina Portions of The Journal of Francis Asbury*. Introductory notes by Grady L.E. Carroll. Nashville: The Parthenon Press, 1964.

Boyd, William K. *The Story of Durham, City of the New South*. Durham: Duke University Press, 1925.

Bradley, Mark L. *This Astounding Close: The Road to Bennett Place*. Chapel Hill: University of North Carolina Press, 2000.

Byrd, William. *Histories of the Dividing Line Betwixt Virginia and North Carolina*, with introduction and notes by William K. Boyd, Ph.D. Raleigh: Historical Commission, 1929.

Clark, Walter, ed. *Histories of the Several Regiments and Battalions from North Carolina in the Great War 1861–1865*. Raleigh: E.M. Uzzell, 1901.

Durden, Robert F. *The Dukes of Durham, 1865-1929*. Durham: Duke University Press, 1987.

Farley, Jennifer. "Socialism & Trade Unions in Durham, North Carolina: 1861 to 1886." *Gold Leaf: News of the Duke Homestead Education and History Corporation 22*. (Fall/Winter 2000-2001).

First Annual Report of the Trustees of the Watts Hospital of Durham, N.C. Durham: The Educator Co., Printers and Publishers, 1896.

Interview with Lawrence Ridgle by Alicia J. Rouvenal. Southern Oral History Program Collection. Southern Historical Collection, Wilson Library, University of North Carolina at Chapel Hill, June 3, 1999.

Jones, Dorothy Phelps. *The End of an Era*. Durham: Brown Enterprises Inc., 2001.

Jones, Southgate. *Glancing Back from the House on Chapel Hill Street: Remembrances of Early Durham*. Oxford, NC: Oxford House Books, 1997.

Kenzer, Robert C. *Kinship and Neighborhood in a Southern Community: Orange County, North Carolina, 1849-1881*. Knoxville: University of Tennessee Press, 1987.

Ketcham, Laura B. " 'This Good Woman:' The Life of Mary Duke Lyon." *Gold Leaf: News of the Duke Homestead Education and History Corporation 24* (Spring 2002).

Knauff, Bob, and Gail Knauff. *Fabric of a Community: The Story of Haw River, North Carolina.* Haw River Historical Association, 1996.

Lawson, John. *A New Voyage to Carolina.* Edited and with an introduction and notes by Hugh Talmadge Lefler. Chapel Hill: University of North Carolina Press, 1967.

Lederer, John. *The Discoveries of John Lederer.* Translated from the Latin by Sir William Talbot. London: 1672.

Paul, Hiram V. *History of the Town of Durham, N.C.,* Raleigh: Edwards, Broughton & Co., Steam Printers and Binders, 1884.

Phillips, Bill,. "Piedmont Country Blues." *Southern Exposure 2* (Spring-Summer 1974).

Renfro, Jean A. "The Role of the Rice: Personal Narrative in Ricer Culture." Master's thesis, University of North Carolina, 1993.

Seeman, Ernest. *American Gold.* New York: Dial Press, 1978.

————. "Hiking in the 1920s: 'Recollections of the Explorers' Club.' " *Eno,* Spring 1976.

Spencer, Cornelia Phillips. *The Last Ninety Days of the War in North Carolina.* New York: Watchman Publishing Co., 1866: reprint ed., Wilmington: Broadfoot Publishing Company, 1993.

Tilley, Nannie M. *The Bright-Tobacco Industry, 1860-1929.* Chapel Hill: University of North Carolina Press, 1948.

Wise, James. "Tugging on Superman's Cape: The Making of a College Legend." *Western Folklore 36* (July 1977).

Yetman, Norman, ed. *Voices from Slavery.* New York: Holt, Rhinehart and Winston, 1970.

INDEX